THE DAY

The day is yours and yours also the night,
    you established the sun and the moon.
It was you who set the boundaries of the earth;
    you made both summer and winter.

Psalm 74:16–17

THE DAY IS YOURS

Slow Spirituality in a
Fast-Moving World

Ian Stackhouse

Paternoster:
thinking faith

MILTON KEYNES ● COLORADO SPRINGS ● HYDERABAD

14 13 12 11 10 09 08   7 6 5 4 3 2 1

First published in 2008 by Paternoster
Paternoster is an imprint of Authentic Media
9 Holdom Avenue, Bletchley, Milton Keynes, Bucks, MK1 1QR
1820 Jet Stream Drive, Colorado Springs, CO 80921, USA
OM Authentic Media, Medchal Road, Jeedimetla Village,
Secunderabad 500 055, A.P., India
www.authenticmedia.co.uk
Authentic Media is a division of IBS-STL U.K., limited by guarantee, with its
Registered Office at Kingstown Broadway, Carlisle, Cumbria CA3 0HA.
Registered in England & Wales No. 1216232. Registered charity 27016

British Library Cataloguing in Publication Data

A catalogue record for this book is available from
the British Library.

ISBN-13 978-1-84227-600-6

Cover design by James Kessell for Scratch the Sky Ltd.
(www.scratchthesky.com)
Print Management by Adare
Printed in Great Britain by J.H. Haynes and Co., Sparkford

Contents

Foreword   vii
Preface   ix

Part One: This is the Day that the Lord Has Made   **1**
1. Gospel Rhythms   3
2. One Day at a Time, Sweet Jesus   16
3. Sabbath Rest   29

   Interlude
   A Sermon on Naboth's Vineyard   43

Part Two: The Liturgy of the Hours   **49**
   Prologue to Part Two   51
4. Your Mercies are New Every Morning   53
5. Practising the Present   64
6. Abide with Me, Fast Falls the Eventide   77

   Interlude
   Praying the Psalms   91

Part Three: Glimpses of the Day   **99**
7. Give Us Today Our Daily Bread   101
8. The Lord's Day   113
9. Time, Space, Rhythm, and Place   126

   Endnotes   138
   Index   155

Foreword

*The Day is Your*s is authored by a busy man thinking his way towards sanity for a civilization. He tells us: 'It seems to me that the battle for civilization will pivot on the outrageously simple challenge of living a day well.' His agenda is simple enough: live one day well and then live another day well. He's right of course.

Ian Stackhouse pastors a busy Baptist Church in a busy part of town with people who lead busy lives. The problem isn't accomplishment. The problem is rushing through our days without noticing that God has given us this one day as a gift. Ian wants us to slow down and taste the grace. Take the time to receive the time. Give the day to God to receive the day as yours. Indeed, the day given to God in simple ways becomes our day. It is a day of freedom to live in the image of God. So how do we do this?

First of all, it won't take you long to realise *The Day is Yours* is not a how-to book, neither is it legalistic. It is written by a learned man with a sensible faith and a deep compassion for the people he serves. He serves real people smack dab in the middle of their lives. He is not insulated from his people by a large staff. He's an old-fashioned pastor that knows his people in person. He is there when they are dying. He can't write legalistically because he couldn't bear to load them with burdens beyond the normal toil of their lives. His people love him to death. He knows for them and for us how expansive a day can be; more like a field of grain than a series of stakes in the ground, and as deep as the bedrock and as high as the sky.

Secondly, if you knew how much Ian accomplishes in a day, as I do, you might think that this is a spiritualised time management scheme. Indeed, I am sure he could write a best-seller on how to get a lot done in a day; although, then again, he couldn't do that because he wouldn't want to lead people into the rush and hurry and raging flood of life that defrauds God of his precious gift to us – this day. On the other hand, I hope he never denies that he is a Type A personality because he most certainly is. His experience of a day is like a great golfer for whom the hole is as big as a basketball hoop. I say this to make the point that Ian is not a monk – he just plans to teach us to go to work like one. As one who has the privilege of knowing both men, Ian reminds me a lot of Eugene Peterson in person and in writing, albeit with an English accent to his syntax.

Ian insists on the recovery of ordinary spirituality! His topics are not new but his treatment is original. You will not feel heavy laden by this book. So he talks about taking one day at a time, the importance of Sabbath, the importance of morning devotions, understanding the wisdom of the liturgy of the hours (for those of us, including himself, who sleep through the night), praying the Lord's Prayer with an extended treatment of the prayer for daily bread. He separates his treatment of the Lord's Day and the Sabbath – well done, thou non-legalistic mystic. (Ian, by the way, along with his four boys, is a sports freak). As for saving civilization, we shouldn't expect a how-to from a guy who can't figure out how to save Burnley FC, his favourite football team. Rather, *The Day is Yours* is remnant spirituality for the ordinary people that save civilizations. In that sense it is pure gospel from the ground up.

Dave Hansen, Senior Pastor, Kenwood Baptist Church, Cincinnati
Author of The Art of Pastoring

Preface

It is very trendy these days to name a child after the place where he or she was conceived. And since creating a book is about as close as a man is going to get to being pregnant, then I guess I ought to call this book Paris; for it was there, in the course of the evening and morning offices at the church of St Gervais, that the idea of a book exploring the spirituality of the day was conceived. All those years ago – somewhere between the gathering darkness of the evening office and the anticipation of daylight that attends the six-thirty morning office – a thought took hold of me, and never left me, which had something to do with the spirituality of a day: 'And there was evening and there was morning, the first day.'[1]

I had read about St Gervais in Michael Marshall's book *Free to Worship*.[2] In a chapter exploring the churchly practice of the daily office, he notes the popularity among Parisians of the three offices of prayer held by the community of Jerusalem at St Gervais – morning, noon and evening – each beginning with half an hour of silence. Following my first visit, which straddled a Friday evening and a Saturday morning, and which I found overwhelming in its charismatic simplicity, St Gervais became for me a parable of the kind of rhythm and contemplation that I believe the Holy Spirit wants to establish in our own communities. Since that time that basic primordial shape, the rhythm of evening and morning, has never left me. It is the ground of what I understand to be the worshipping life of the church; and, as such, brackets what I offer here as a spirituality of the day.

Strangely enough I have undertaken the writing of this book, more often than not, in the early hours of the morning, somewhere between the passing of the night and the arrival of the dawn light. Without being too romantic, it was as if the book decided to shape itself around the liturgy of the hours, the morning office in particular. That's just the way it was. So if the thought processes seem a bit muddled, you now know why. It was not as if I was unable to write in the daytime; nor that my church refused me space to think. On the contrary, I have been very fortunate to pastor churches that have truly believed in the importance of theological reflection and the need for their pastor to write. The people at Millmead would have had no problem with me writing during my working hours. It is simply that the creative juices with this book seemed to flow with the daily call of the Psalmist to awaken the dawn.

Unlike my first book, *The Gospel-Driven Church*, this book is not only more accessible, I hope, but also much more of a collaborative project. I have been keen to receive feedback from the start rather than simply at the end of the process. Due acknowledgement and thanks must go therefore to a number of people, not least Peter Jackson, Mike Pusey and Ant Horton – my pastoral team at Millmead – who suffered extracts of this book in our Tuesday morning staff meetings. The conversations that ensued were invaluable to me in the final shaping of the book, even as their fellowship over these past few years has been invaluable in the shaping of my life. It is with their permission that I write so freely about the difficulties many of us have in actually entering into the Sabbath day. My insistence that they as ministers of the gospel take seriously the call to Sabbath-day rest is more than matched by their insistence that I take it seriously too.

I also want to thank various others at Millmead and beyond, such as Rob Marshall, Karen Case-Green, Simon Walsh, Dean Sanders, Rachel Burn, Andy Burton, and Julie Chamek, who read early drafts of the book and made some very important remarks in relationship to their own everyday settings. After all, there is no point developing a spirituality that works only for clergy types. It is critical for me that this book works at the level of everyday life: bringing up children, commuting to work, going to lectures, making friends. And what each one of them provided, in their own unique way, was a necessary filter for some of my less practical insights. That the book might still be unrealistic is not their fault but mine, but I am grateful all the same for their time and encouragement, not to mention the support of my PA, Sara Sims, whose untiring efforts to create space for me to attend to my vocation – as well as her ability to track down books and references with incredible speed – are greatly appreciated.

One unexpected blessing during the final editing of the book was the chance to meet up with Eugene and Jan Peterson at their home in Lakeside, Montana during a family holiday last summer. Having seen first-hand the wildness of where he lives, I can understand better his frustration with so much of contemporary North American culture. Montana has a spiritual geography all of its own. And during our brief visit I was able to thank him personally for all he has written over the years. As will be evident from the book (and I am sure I speak on behalf of countless others at this point), I owe Eugene a huge debt. Indeed I seem to quote him everywhere – the reason being that not only did his books on pastoral ministry save me from the corrosive and crippling effects of church growth books, but they also began to shape in me what I write about here: a rhythm of prayer and attentiveness to God in the actual setting of place, family and congregation. So it is with grateful thanks that I acknowledge his work.

I am also most grateful to Robin Parry at Paternoster for his constant encouragement and enthusiasm; and greatly indebted to Kate Kirkpatrick for her assiduous and often reflective editing of the text.

Finally, as always, my special thanks go to Susanna, my beautiful wife, and our four wonderful sons – John, Tim, Benedict, and Daniel – with whom we share our lives. Our life together as a family is really what constitutes *daily* discipleship for me. It is there in the routines of our lives together that we learn to live each day with fidelity, perseverance, gratitude, forgiveness, joy, and – above all else – love. If daily spirituality doesn't work there this book is simply ink on paper. And though Dad loves his solitude, and though sometimes he dreams of escaping to the mountains for the day, I will never forget little Daniel's early morning incursions into my study during the writing of this book. They remind me that discipleship is not about being alone with the Alone, to quote the mystics, but about persons in communion.

Ian Stackhouse

PART ONE:

THIS IS THE DAY THAT THE LORD HAS MADE

1

Gospel Rhythms

In the morning light the city had a look of a face fresh from a spell of crying, purged of all passion.[1]

Ever felt you were dropped in the wrong century? I have. And over the years I have met many others who have felt similarly. So much of what constitutes modern living passes us by. We just can't see what all the hype is about. Everyone is cheering, but, as far as we are concerned, the Emperor has no clothes. The only thing I can think is that the proverbial stork made a big mistake.

I first suspected it a few years ago at a weekend gathering of friends at one of these leisure parks that are so popular. Although the facilities were superb – ideal for young children – there was something disturbingly odd about spending a weekend in an artificially conceived wooded area, the purpose of which was to help me 'get away from it all'. It felt like something off *The Truman Show*.[2] Even the squirrels seemed unreal. By Sunday morning, in the absence of congregational worship, this idyllic, sylvan retreat was starting to make me feel very claustrophobic.

Maybe I am too intense about these things. Why not relax and simply accept it for what it is? Which, I am glad to say, I did – much to the relief of my long-suffering wife, who has had to deal with my existential crises on more than one occasion. On reflection, however, at a later time, I recanted. It occurred to me that theme parks and their popularity among the middle classes are indeed symptomatic of a major problem in our modern society: namely, a disconnection from the ordinary rhythms of life. The notion of three days 'getting away from it all' in order for us to survive is precisely what happens when we lose our rhythm. As

Walter Brueggemann so creatively discerns, the modern weekend
– with its endless sport, entertainment and shopping – is in many
ways an indictment of modern living: a form of escapism (and,
more specifically, a way of avoiding the nitty-gritty of the
church's own three day story of Good Friday, Holy Saturday and
Easter Sunday).[3] The modern weekend bears the symptoms of
the chronic sickness in our fast-paced society, where even leisure
must be justified by the dictates of the market. But so authorita-
tive has the weekend become that even Christians find nothing
wrong in regularly fleeing to the holiday cottage on a Friday
evening, thus avoiding the painstaking and often lacklustre work
of community building.

The answer is not to reintroduce a strict Sabbath, nor, for that
matter, to frown upon members of the congregation who go away
for the weekend. For me, the oft-cited image of John Calvin worshipping with the saints on a Sunday morning and playing skit-
tles in the afternoon is about as good a definition of the Sabbath as
you can find. Furthermore, lest my readers already regard me as
a social prig, I also like to get away from it all. But why the leisure
thing is so illustrative is because the churchly concept of rest is
rooted not in some consumer exchange, where we have to get
something out of even our leisure time, but rooted instead in the
gritty, particular and local setting of a Christian community in
which playing and praying together takes on the nature of gift. In
fact, the very essence of Christian salvation is grounded in the
actual stuff of incarnation. There is nothing neat or artificial about
it. To try to escape from its messiness, its mundanity and its
rhythms, as so many are now seeking to do, is therefore nothing
less than apostasy. It is a sign that we have given up trying to live
well, in the stuff of daily living, and have opted instead for a simulated world.

Remember the Good Old Days

I do realise that all of this could sound hopelessly romantic as
well as overdone. I am susceptible, I admit, to nostalgia. I am one
of those sad characters who drones on about the good old days
when footballers were real men, with proper jerseys and proper

boots (and anyone caught wearing an Alice Band would simply have been laughed at). However, there was undoubtedly something about those days that was refreshingly simple, where we celebrated the joy of doing something simply for the love of it – what we might call the cult of the amateur.[4]

These days, we inhabit a very different world. It is a regime of targets, performance and management where, even as young as three years old, our lives are assessed for their utility. Gone is the notion of leisurely time (even if we still retain the concept of leisure). Instead we justify our busyness with what we now call quality time. But our kids are not fooled. They want quantity time, and lots of it, and the only time they seem to get that is precious holiday time; whereupon, lazing somewhere around a pool, and finally enjoying the company of those we love, we wonder why on earth we live as we do. As it says so boldly on a boundary fence cum wayside pulpit just off the M40, daubed in white paint for the benefit of passing London commuters: 'Why do I still do this every day?'

Consequently, every August, returning from holiday, disembarking from the ferry at Dover, and joining the motorway traffic, we convince ourselves that this time we really are going to crack this busyness thing. Renewed by two weeks away on the continent – the second week of which we actually started to feel half human again – we lug ourselves down to the local bookshop to buy the latest thing on time management, convinced that this year things are going to be different. And whilst we do make some incremental changes, and one or two adjustments, nothing really changes. In the secular calendar, which is: 'Back to school in September, Tax returns end of September, October half-term, Bonfire night, School Play rehearsal, Christmas shopping' (this is the agreed liturgical calendar in my neck of the woods), by mid-December we are near to burn-out once again; the reason being that for all our good intentions and little changes we never actually put the axe to the root of the tree.

That is why I refuse to read books on time management. The very notion of time management, it seems to me at least, is actually part of the problem and why nothing ever seems to change. As if we could manage time? It is an admission of defeat before we have even started. It is a concession to the creed that life is indeed a series of schedules to be adhered to rather than a rhythm of grace to dance to. And what could be more soul-destroying than that? For sure, we need to make appointments. It is unlikely, in my day at least, that we will return to the kind of ad hoc, drop round, 'playing up the street till tea-time' culture that even I enjoyed as a kid; leisure and friendship have become far too serious and planned for that kind of serendipity. And to the extent that I want to keep my job and be known as someone who is punctual, I too am happy to keep a diary. Even so, the idea that I am shaped by my schedules has become so abhorrent to me over the past few years that I am now ready to explore, with others who have the courage, a different way of living that is more consistent with the rhythms of God's creation rather than the hourly news bulletin; a way of life more attuned to the prayerful liturgy of the hours than the computer Day-timer; an experience of daily living that is more to do with immersion in daily rituals than adherence to schedules.

The odds are stacked against us. White noise pervades the atmosphere, and the neon lights of the city push back the darkness. The 24/7 world is now fully upon us. The coherence and integrity of a world in which 'there was evening, and there was morning, the first day,' has been ripped asunder by the corporate giants, laying claim to the earth with their compelling images, branding everyone and everything with their cool logos.[5] In fact, so greatly have we violated the order of God's good creation that there will be some in this present generation who will live their whole lives out of sync with the natural order of things: so pre-occupied that they will never hear the sound of the nightingale, nor ever smell the intoxicating scent of the night jasmine, simply because there is no night anymore. Indeed, it may well be that the notion of a Sabbath – one day among seven decidedly different to the others – will never return to mainstream culture, with those who are inclined to stop once in a while, out of sheer exhaustion, simply ridiculed for their inefficiency.

My sense, even so, is that there are some survivors from before the great cataclysm who still remember what it was like to live in a real world without simulation: a world where you didn't have to queue for an hour at a theme park to take a plastic boat on an artificial lake, but where you could jump into a wooden punt, on an actual lake, with real water, and mess around to your heart's content until the mysterious colours of dusk told you it was time to go home.[6] I remember it well. And the time has come, I believe, to call a stop: to enact before a jaded, over-sated, noise-filled generation, the sounds and the symbols of that lost world. As sociologist Harvey Cox comments in his discussion on the loss of festivity and fantasy in modern life: 'Unable to conjure up fantasy images on our own, we have given over the field to mass production. Walt Disney and his imitators have populated it with virtuous mice and friendly skunks. Low-grade cinema and formula-TV producers have added banal symbols and predictable situations.'[7] This is my conviction too. It is the world we live in. But now a unique opportunity presents itself to the church to oppose such banality with the creative genius of an unhindered Christian imagination.

The Death of a Culture

Such a proposal, I am aware, seems a bit late in the day. The horse has already bolted. In seeking to pull back the years, to reclaim a sense of created order amidst this chaos of modern gadgetry, there is every danger we could be seen as nothing more than Luddites, even by our Christian contemporaries. What has boating on a lake got to do with the Kingdom of God, for goodness' sake? That is to confuse the Kingdom of God with the myth of a golden age; and in any case, Christendom has gone, or so they tell us. Any idea that we can retrieve the neighbourhood is simply misguided. The world has changed forever.

But is this really the case? To be sure, computers are here to stay. Me and my 'Bring back the quill' friends realised long ago that we were on to a loser. Furthermore, I will be the first to admit that the assumptions upon which our churches did mission now have to be rethought. Post-modernity is not simply an academic indulgence, but a social and cultural reality. Nevertheless, there is vestige enough of the past to piece together a Christian faith that is classical even as it is contemporary: in short, a Christian faith that avoids what we might term a pious rear-guard action, or a pastiche, but at the same time goes beyond the superficiality of mission based solely on the notion of cultural relevance.

Indeed, there is nothing more important now for the Christian church than to embark upon this spiritual task, for Western culture is showing every sign of being in its death throes. We are witnessing the twilight years of a major civilisation; the new Dark Age is nearly upon us.[8] When hotels open for dogs, as they have done recently in California, with en suite facilities in every room, remote control television, and an *à la carte* menu we know that cultural decadence is fast approaching its end-point;[9] when multi-culturalism means that one cannot even state 'the bleeding obvious' for fear of reprisals, we know that we are not far off politically correct fascism;[10] when a whole nation is coerced by the media into mourning the death of the Queen of Hearts, Princess Diana, when – truth be told – we hardly knew her, we know that sentimentality has begun to reign.[11]

What the church must offer as an alternative is not its own brand of sentimental pietism. Sadly, in times of crisis, that is often the only response the church can muster, and it doesn't take long before it finally capitulates to the prevailing culture, as in Germany in the 1930s. Rather, what the church needs at this present time is something akin to what St Benedict offered as he saw pagan culture collapse under the weight of its own moral decadence: namely a new kind of monasticism that preserves, through small committed cadres of believers, what we might call the classical tradition. As Alistair MacIntyre put it so poignantly at the end of *After Virtue*: 'We are waiting not for Godot but for another – doubtless very different – St. Benedict.'[12]

What this book sets out to do is give expression to that instinct in the form of a Christian spirituality which, although it may look pretty aimless with its love for slowness, could possibly be the most radical, if not prophetic, action the church could take at such a time of cultural crisis. In the end, early morning prayer, praying the psalms, keeping the Sabbath and Lord's Day worship – the kind of things we will be exploring throughout the book – could be the very means by which the Christian tradition might survive during this period, and the basis upon which a new civilisation might arise, simply by getting us to pay attention to something bigger than ourselves. We live, after all, in one of the most narcissistic ages. We are obsessed with Self. But our pretentious visions of the future have left us anxious and without hope.

Living in the fast-track means that we are never really present for anything.

This came home to me on one occasion recently when I visited the Orangerie in Paris to view the huge *Water Lilies*, or *Nymphéas* as they are called, painted by Monet. They are indeed incredible canvases, and are meant to be received as a meditation on the eternal mysteries of the world. Approaching something like abstract art, cumulatively the *Nymphéas* express, through the variations of daylight hours upon the same subject, what can only be understood as spiritual timelessness.[13] In that sense the two adjoining rooms of the Orangerie that house the eight canvases are less art gallery than monastic cloister, and should be treated as such.[14] The paintings are contemplations on the eternal present – a theme that often emerges when the artist tethers himself to a liturgy of the hours. At the very least there ought to be silence. Instead what we have are crowds of noisy tourists, digital and video cameras in hand, pausing for no more than five seconds before moving on to the souvenir shop.

Whilst this observation may simply be artistic snobbery on my part, my conviction is that it is an accurate description of the current sickness in our world: a consumerism that promises the earth but delivers restlessness or rootlessness instead. For all its glossy images of the good life, we never actually seem to inhabit any one of them. They are simply illusions. Living a day well, however – living it prayerfully, contentedly and gratefully – sets us firmly within the grand vision of Christian faith, and opens up to us the transcendent possibilities of even the most mundane moments of our day. 'Making tea becomes a treat. Travelling to work an adventure. Cooking a meal a voyage of discovery. Eating it a perilous pleasure.'[15] Once we slow down, let go of the future, and stop orchestrating our own success, even a trip round the supermarket can become a march down the aisles of 'Glory' with my left foot and 'Amen' with my right. Well, sometimes, at least.

Attentive Spirituality

My suspicion, if not thesis, is that if sufficient numbers of people can live like this – Christians, to be sure – we could have something approaching a revolution on our hands. The kingdoms of this world could indeed become the kingdoms of our Lord and Christ, not by way of some huge divine intervention, but simply by the believing community maintaining a distinctively Christian identity and performing distinctive Christian practices. This is not to say, of course, that there is no place for the supernatural. Christianity is supernatural from start to finish. What kind of Christianity would we be talking about if it were not heavily vested with supernatural power from on high? But sometimes in the history of God's people what is required more than anything is not a revival, nor a pious exuberance, but a deepening consciousness – an imaginative attentiveness to the grace that 'This is the Day that the Lord has made, we will rejoice and be glad in it.' *The Day is Yours* is an exploration of just such a spirituality.

The Day is Yours makes no claims to success. It may be dismissed by some as contemplative wistfulness. Indeed, in seeking to recover a more classical spirituality we must register this concern. As Bonnie J. Miller-McLemore points out, there are already too many books on spirituality written by contemplative types, usually celibate males, when what is urgently needed is a spirituality for the masses: for the extroverts, for the working mother, for business people.[16] She has a point (although I ought to remind the reader that I am a married man with four sons). Even so, whether one is extrovert or introvert, activist or mystic, it is my genuine conviction that the battle for Western civilisation will be won by these little daily victories by the people of God.

The Day is Yours is not, I hope, a miscellany of pious meditations conceived down by the lakeside. I would like it to be received, if possible, as a subversive rear-guard action – a protest if you will – against the trivialisation of culture, and the violation of time. The popularity of television programmes like *The Monastery* is no surprise to me. The culture is desperate to rediscover our sense of wonder. And what the monastic tradition is offering us at the moment, through its liturgy of the hours, is a subversion of clock-time – its deadlines, its agendas, its obsession with numbers – offering instead an alternative rendering of the world in which we pay attention to even the most basic human activities and gestures. After all, the real contrast in Christian discipleship is not so much between contemplation and activism –

the Mary and Martha story being the usual example[17] – but between attentiveness and distraction. One can be a contemplative, presumably, and be thoroughly stressed out, or a high achiever but working deeply from the centre of one's baptismal identity as one who is loved by God in Jesus Christ. The issue is not how much one does, or how little, but the manner in which one does it. It just so happens, however, that among the few people at the moment who seem to be trying to work this out practically are those ensconced within the confines of the monastery. Rather like the monks of the mid-third century who sought to escape the corruption of a degrading empire by retreating to the desert, it is left, once again, to those outside the institutional church to act as the vanguard of renewal by offering an alternative to the idolatry of modern technology and the tyranny of time.[18]

Kairos and *Chronos* Time

It is worth noting how the monastics do this, because it is not immediately apparent to those unfamiliar with this tradition. From the outside, the day-time schedule of the average monk looks terrifying. Anyone who has made a few days retreat to a monastery will know the fear that grips the heart when you are shown to your room (or should I say cell), given the time of the offices, and then left to yourself. Having just come from the world of frenetic activity the day seems to stretch out interminably. It takes at least a couple of days to slow down, hand over the mobile phone, and even begin to enter into the rhythm of the place.[19] But that is the point. The liturgy of the hours, expressed in the various offices of the day, is not a schedule but a rhythm. An hour, such as the hour of morning prayer (called Lauds) or the hour of evening prayer (called Vespers), is not so much a unit of chronology as a mood of the soul.[20] The coming of the light, for instance, the silence of the house as others are perhaps still asleep, the anticipation of the day ahead, the fact that it is only one day – thank God – and not a series of days to contend with, all combine in what we call the hour of morning. When it begins and when it ends is debatable – although surely in the setting of a monastery it will end, as Lauds gives way to Prime. But for those of us who do not inhabit the monastery and find ourselves on the train to London, or taking the children to school, approaching a day through the concept of the hours affords the possibility of responding attentively and consciously to the particular nuance of each season of the day, rather than wishing we were somewhere else.

Clock time, after all, is a fairly modern construct. There is nothing sacrosanct about minutes and seconds (although the way punctuality is deemed a virtue in Western societies suggests that clocks may as well be regarded as wayside shrines). More than that, time can be a tyrant. Time can dictate us in ways that rob us of present enjoyment. Anyone wanting to engage in Christian mission in this next century is, one way or other, going to have to wrestle with this, as Os Guinness so forcibly points out.[21] It is not a question of mere semantics. The qualitative difference between clock time and the Christian concept of the hours is a very real one. It is the difference between *chronos* and *kairos*: between time that is merely accounted for in terms of schedules versus time that speaks of opportunity; between time that is respected and time that is entered into; between time that is hurried and time that is enjoyed.

We see this same reverence for mood as opposed to chronology in a slightly larger frame in Ecclesiastes, where the preacher exhorts the faithful to respect that there is 'a time for everything, and a season for every activity under heaven'.[22] So familiar are we with this poem that it has ended up as something fairly innocuous. But what the Preacher is alluding to is the vital knowledge that life consists not simply of individual days but of a number of seasons, or moods, and the art of living is to discern the time and then embrace it wholeheartedly. If it is a time to weep then we should weep; if it is a time to laugh then we should laugh. If it is a time to embrace, to take another example, then we had better get on and embrace; if it is a time to refrain, then, with all due reverence, stop; for to violate the time that one lives in, to fail to appreciate the mood of life one is passing through, is to live inappropriately. And for a Christian civilisation to survive in this increasingly fast world, we will have to retrieve this concept of time.

The Day is Yours, I hope, will make a contribution in that direction, and offer some practical ways ahead. It seems to me that the battle for civilisation will pivot on the outrageously simple challenge of living a day well. It begins where every new day begins, of course, with the light of the dawn and the call to early morning prayer, for as Dietrich Bonhoeffer once remarked, 'The early morning belongs to the church of the Risen Christ.'[23] If we are to live a day well, then some attention at least must be given to the kind of things we do when we first awake. Furthermore, similar attention needs to be given to the things we say, do and reflect upon last thing at night, hence a chapter on the spirituality of sleep in chapter 6. Between those two sequences of the day, I want to explore what it is to live a day gratefully, contentedly and prayerfully, and see this in the present context as something quite subversive: a return to the liturgy of creation in Genesis, culminating in the seventh day when the Lord rested from his work. For daily living in the ordered rhythms of 'and there was evening and there was morning', as opposed to the dehumanising, chaotic rhythms of the modern world, bears witness to the fact that this is God's world, and can only be lived well if it is understood as God's world. Indeed what is the proclamation of the Kingdom of God but a recovery, to some extent at least, of this divine aesthetic – the new creation of Christ – and an anticipation of that world to come, the Sabbath rest of God? In which case, some attention needs to be given to what theologians call the eschatological implications of all of this; for the more I have pondered these things, and tried to live them, the more I have become aware that the discipline that goes into living a day well, a Sabbath day in particular, is a kind of rehearsal for that world to come. To live a day well is to get a glimpse into living eternity well. In fact my argument in chapter 8 concerning the Lord's Day is that church worship is precisely that: not simply a chance for Christians to meet, but, incredible as it might sound, a glimpse of that world to come. It is this that I want to explore fully in the final chapter, thus making the bold suggestion that to live any day well, not just the Lord's Day, is in fact to see eternity in an hour. By paying attention to a day we are in effect treating with utmost seriousness the claim that Christian existence at its most basic and mundane level is a foretaste of, if not participation in, future realities.

Living on a Four-count Rhythm

Since the issues we now face in our high-tech world are not going to disappear, my guess is that if we fail to redeem the time, fail to recover the day, then life will become ever more frenetic and ever more meaningless. As Quentin Schultze so clearly puts it: 'If we are not able to slow down enough to discover moral wisdom, our high-tech endeavours will create ever more diversionary noise, resulting in thinner lives.'[24] Dorothy Bass evocatively elaborates on this theme: 'Remote from the natural world and wired into a workplace that never shuts down, we are in danger of slipping into an existence that is always winter and never Christmas.'[25] And why it is critical for us to confront this in the church is because, in a very real sense, time has already been redeemed. Indeed, the whole narrative of the Christian gospel can be read as redemption of time. To state it technically, the entropy of catastrophic time has been redeemed by the kairic time of Jesus Christ, heralding the great prophetic or eschatological time of the new heaven and the new earth.[26] But what the Christian community is now called upon to bear witness to is that new creation time, through the cadences and rhythms of the new time. In a world of ever-increasing speed, the vocation of the church is to keep proper time. To live as anxiously and as fast as the world is to deny this new time and pretend that it never took place; to live with a sense of *kairos* time is to live as a true believer.

How we do this is a delicate exercise, and partly what this book seeks to negotiate (although I am keen to avoid a 'How-to' approach). The simple thing would be to retreat to the mountains, and let the solitude and space do it for us. But, sadly, things are not as easy as that. Short of a dramatic change in circumstances, most of us will have to work this out in the pressure cooker of modern suburban life. We may holiday in the mountains – as I have done this summer with my family in Montana – but the world most of us have to return to is not nearly so silent or spectacular.

However, it is from the mountains, in the wisdom of Norman Maclean's novel *A River Runs Through It*, that we receive an important clue as to where the truth lies. Part novel, part what seems to be a meditation on the eternal verities of fly-fishing,

Maclean recounts the story of his childhood: fishing the Big Blackfoot river in Montana with his brother Paul and tutored by his father – a Presbyterian minister – in the art of casting on what he calls 'a four count rhythm, between ten and two o'clock.' Anyone who has fly-fished, as I did with my own father when I was a child, will know the merits of this approach. Furthermore they will know that fly-fishing in its purest form is simply a metaphor for eternity itself. As Maclean notes: 'Poets talk about "spots of time", but it is really fishermen who experience eternity compressed into a moment. No one can tell what a spot of time is until suddenly the whole world is a fish and the fish is gone.'[27]

How true that is. But since fly-fishing is a metaphor, then it makes sense for Maclean to observe further that his father's insistence on the four count rhythm was in fact an insistence that all of life is a rhythm – or should be. 'As a Scot and a Presbyterian, my father believed that man was by nature a mess and had fallen from an original state of grace,' notes Maclean. 'Somehow I early developed the notion that he had done this by falling from a tree. As for my father, I never knew whether he believed God was a mathematician but he certainly believed God could count and that only by picking up God's rhythms were we able to regain power and beauty. Unlike many Presbyterians, he often used the word "beautiful".'[28]

It is my desire, now that I am in my mid-life, to live by such a rhythm; to render life as something beautiful to God. In order to do so we must protest against this 24/7 world with a counter-rhythm that takes seriously the gift of each and every day, as well as the necessity of one day out of seven for life other than work. It is to these two features of daily spirituality that we now turn, before exploring in Part Two the rhythm of a day set to the liturgy of the hours.

2

One Day at a Time, Sweet Jesus

If anyone would come after me, he must deny himself and take up his cross daily and follow me.[1]

I have a cartoon picture on the notice board in my study of a rather bedraggled looking woman with hair all over the place and huge bags under her eyes. Under the cartoon is the caption: 'I try to take one day at a time. Lately a number have hit me all at once.' Everyone who sees it laughs. They know exactly how she feels. Life can often be completely overwhelming. But at least she tried. As Jesus said to his disciples, seeking to counsel them against the prevailing anxiety of a world without God, 'Therefore, do not worry about tomorrow, for tomorrow will worry about itself. Each day has enough trouble of its own.'[2] In this chapter I would like to explore this 'one day at a time' concept and place it at the centre of contemporary Christian discipleship. 'One day at a time' living is Jesus' simple but profound counsel to sophisticated moderns on how to survive, and although it runs the risk of appearing naïve, it has enough adherents to make it a bestseller in the 'How to' market.

To live one day at a time is no guarantee of anything, of course. The trouble with life is precisely that: it is daily. But at least by paying attention to just one day at a time there is a sporting chance that we just might make it through. To take one day at a time is to intentionally and wilfully shut out the horizon of all subsequent days in order to focus on the unique challenges of this day. It is to recognise that tomorrow, in one sense, never comes, and therefore is not worth worrying about.[3]

This is easier said than done. Days have a knack of piling up on top of one another, as our poor sufferer in the cartoon complains, so that soon enough life overwhelms us with the anxiety of unfinished jobs, unresolved conflicts and unpredictable kids. Things may be peaceful at the moment, but who can account for the prospect of rising interest rates or unruly teenagers, to give just a couple of examples. The knack of one-day spirituality, however, rests in the knowledge, to use a more antiquated translation and adaptation of Jesus' words, ' "that sufficient unto the day is the evil thereof," and most assuredly, if we possess faith, sufficient also, will be the good.'[4] When those days arrive, God will be there. As Jesus says to the disciples, in the rather different context of having to give an account before the authorities, 'Do not worry about what to say or how to say it. At that time you will be given what to say.'[5] When those teenage years arrive, and we as parents will be called to the reckoning, God will be there, and 'you will be given what to say'.

Therefore, since this really is the case, then tomorrow, in one sense, can be filed away, both emotionally and existentially. We cannot deal now with what will happen then. All we can do is enter into the realities of this day, believing that grace will fill it. The only day I can existentially commit to is today. This is the only day we can live. Tomorrow will arrive, sure enough. The problems it will present have the power to render us speechless. But God promises to be there. For now, I am called to embrace this day: its uniqueness, its shape, its context, and its boundaries. God's unit is a day.

I think I would say, as someone who has chosen to pursue my vocational call in the area of spiritual theology rather than purely academic theology, this 'one day at a time' spirituality is just about the most important feature of Christian formation. Not that we pastors slap this wisdom upon any and every situation, for then it would cease to be wisdom; it would simply end up as a platitude – something pastors have a special predilection for. What I mean is that in listening to the struggles and concerns of parishioners I have become very aware that living one day at a time is a common practice among Christians and ought to be made more of by those of us who are seeking to cultivate practical discipleship in our churches. Whether it is anxiety about children, waiting for confirmation of a diagnosis, or recovery from debt or alcohol, often the only way ahead is to take, as the pop song goes, 'One Day at a Time, Sweet Jesus'.

Of course, it was incredible to us teenagers back in the seventies that such lyrics could ever make the pop charts, let alone number one in the Hit Parade. In my secular childhood it was one of the few times I had even heard the name of Jesus, let alone heard it sung on *Top of the Pops*. But that it did achieve record sales, and that for a brief moment Lena Martell was more popular than the Bay City Rollers, is testimony to the fact that both outside and inside the church people know that life is only possible in one-day increments.

Whether, as the song concludes, 'It's worse now,' than when Jesus 'walked among men,' is a moot point. In one sense, human nature has always been the same, although I guess one of the motivations behind my own thinking is that the culture we inhabit is degenerating at a fast pace. But whether it is worse, or whether things have always been this bad, her sentiment is right:

> Yesterday's gone sweet Jesus,
> And tomorrow may never be mine.
> Lord help me today, show me the way.
> One day at a time.[6]

Yes there are strategies to contemplate, long-term plans to consider, decisions to be made. We cannot avoid these. We cannot bury our heads in the sand. But in terms of survival, just about the most we can manage at the emotional level is one day. And when we have done one day, maybe then, and only then, will we be able to do another. A student of ours has a Post-It note stuck on her notice board which says it perfectly: 'Lord, I'll take care of today and you take care of tomorrow, and by the time I get to tomorrow, you would have already taken care of my today.'

For those of us who live at the melancholic end of the personality spectrum this is good news: a practical way through the kind of troughs that such a personality type is vulnerable to. During a particularly bad bout of depression a friend of mine went through, it was the discipline of living one day at a time, he told me, which brought him through. Basically, he would wake up each morning, ask Jesus if we can do today – *we* being the operative word – and then, having received some kind of affirmation from the Lord that indeed it was possible to do today, he proceeded to live the day. Then the next day he would do exactly the same thing. Waking in the morning, usually from not too good a sleep and then, having received some kind of affirmation that, yes, we can do today, he would proceed to get up to begin the day; and then the next day, and the next day, and the next day. He got through. As he describes it, it was a one-day contract.

The Fellowship of the Wounded

I am aware in referring to my friend's struggle with depression that not a lot of popular theology is written from this perspective. It is too intent on avoiding pain rather than embracing it; of seeking to ignore depression rather than understand it; and what it means for spiritual theology is tantamount to light confectionery. Classical spiritual formation, of the kind that stands the test of time, more often than not emerges from times of great trial, and to be always looking to circumvent these formative times by recourse to a crude triumphalism only serves to consign Christian experience to the foothills. As a pastor who visits the members of his congregation, I have to say that my most vivid experiences of the presence of God have been in the presence of suffering.

So it comes as no surprise to me that wintry days, as opposed to sunny days, are precisely the context in which great faith arises. Anxiety about the future, as Jesus is most keenly aware of, is the breeding ground of the very thing we are seeking to recover from: namely, the discipline of living one day at a time.

Never more is this the case than with the uncertainties surrounding cancer. Frequently in pastoral ministry we are called to journey with those who are struggling in one way or another with cancer – whether it is early diagnosis, trips to the hospital for chemotherapy, periods of remission, or, sometimes, the final stages of terminal illness. Such occurrences in people's lives provide some of the most challenging spiritual encounters for those seeking to bring assurance and comfort. I never get used to it. Each visit to the hospital or the home is absolutely unique and no amount of pastoral experience or theological skill is ever really adequate. In fact, sometimes it gets in the way. So desperate are we to alleviate suffering that we end up, if we are not careful, sermonising at the bedside. But it is here, listening to the stories of those going through the valley of the shadow of death, rather than trying to fix them, that one very quickly becomes aware that for this person in front of me life has become the simple exercise of taking one day at a time. Faced with the prospect of long-term chemotherapy, probable hair loss and possible secondaries, one day is about as much as human emotions can cope with. Tomorrow is all too unpredictable.

What is noticeable among this special fellowship of the broken is the sheer doggedness by which this is applied. One day at a time is not a nice coffee-shop meditation, or a lifestyle choice, but a ruthless determination to take the commands of Jesus seriously. The alternative is unthinkable. The cost of living in tomorrow is so high emotionally that one-day Christianity becomes a matter of life and death. But in the process of this high-risk living something beautiful happens that becomes a sacrament of life. It is the old story. Finitude is the breeding ground for hope. How many times do we hear from those in the fellowship of the suffering how uncertainty about life somehow gathers the vitality of the future into the present, so that each one day takes on a richness hitherto unimagined. Bad days apart – for I am not so romantic, or idealistic, to suggest that every day will be like this – there is enough data out there to confirm that this is very often the experience for those with cancer. It is as if the awareness of possible death shortens the horizon of the many days ahead so as to focus on the gift of this day. Being able, finally, to number one's days aright, does indeed give a heart of wisdom, as the Psalmist promises,[7] so that we finally see each day for what it is, entering into it with thanksgiving.

In that sense it has long struck me that people wrestling with cancer, other serious illnesses, or even mental health problems, are living more biblically than the rest of us. Here we all are, rushing about, frantically seeking to avail ourselves of everything the culture is offering us, hardly being present for any of it; and here on the other hand is a fellowship of the suffering who are learning to suck the juice out of each day, giving thanks for something as simple as a smile. I witnessed this most vividly in a dear friend of mine, Katie, whom I used to visit at her house in Farnham during the last stages of cancer. Katie was only thirty-six and had been receiving treatment for a rare cancer over the previous two years. She was propped up in a bed her husband Ciarán had lovingly set up for her near the window, overlooking the garden.

On one occasion when I visited, it was early evening, and as I sat there in the quiet, not wanting to fill the space with pastoral pleasantries, I noticed that Katie had become transfixed by the sight of a blue tit feeding off the bird table just outside. I have no way of knowing if I am right, but for Katie it was as if the past, the future, and the present had all concertinaed into that one ful-filled moment, where somewhere in a Surrey village a tiny avian creature was employing all its skills to wrestle a nut from the birdfeeder in the sight of a young woman dying of cancer. Katie's whole demeanour was filled with gratitude and praise. As Annie Dillard puts it in her journal, describing the spectacular flight of a hummingbird that she chanced upon one day: 'The answer must be, I think, that beauty and grace are performed whether or not we will or sense them. The least we can do is try to be there.'[8]

For Katie, the awareness of her own finitude made her present for more of those graces than would otherwise have been the case, which is why visiting the sick or the terminally ill is so often a rich experience for those in pastoral ministry. The prospect of death created in her an intensity of living, a greediness for life, a joy in affliction. And for those of us who are allowed in on those times, people like Katie become our teachers in learning to live gratefully – one day at a time. Life is not meant to be a sprint, see-ing how many goodies we can acquire on the way. Rather it is to be lived slowly. Just as good food demands to be eaten slowly, the pallet delighting in the sensations of a leisurely meal, so life is meant to be taken slowly.[9]

Again, this does not mean that activists must therefore become contemplatives; nor that extroverts must become introverts. This call to live one day at a time has little to do with personality alter-ation. An extrovert is an extrovert, and an introvert is an intro-vert, as far as I am concerned. Christian spirituality is not about violating the personality, any more than it is about escaping into sacred spaces. But what an authentic Christian spirituality insists upon is the importance of receiving life as a gift; of not missing life in a flurry of meaningless activity. It is about entering into a day attentively and gratefully, as opposed to arrogantly and anxiously, of living deeply as well as widely. It may well be that we will go to this city or that city, do a little business. Who knows? There is nothing wrong with making plans. But when we grasp at it, we need to hear again the wisdom of James who reminds us our life is just a mist. Rather than laying hold of our unknown tomorrows, we ought to say 'if it is the Lord's will,'[10] entering instead into the unique challenges that this day presents us.[11]

The tragedy of the rich fool in Jesus' parable was not so much that he died and was thus unable to enjoy his wealth, but that whilst he did live his pursuit of greater and bigger barns prevented him from enjoying the real things of life.[12] For in the end life does not consist in the abundance of things, but in daily gratitude for the simple things. Surprisingly (or maybe not so surprisingly) it was the tragedy of 9/11 that opened up the possibility for this kind of living. As Kathleen Norris observed, 'if the terrorists' intent was to destroy us, they failed miserably. And we succeeded in finding a measure of grace. A more unified country, at least for a time. No riots, no panicked runs on banks. We were a more thoughtful people, if only briefly. We enjoyed the grace of a week without the usual bombardment of advertisements, a week without celebrity trivia.'

I am told the same thing happened during the war: instead of worrying about trivia, with the war came a new intensity of living that enriched rather than diminished people's lives. Suddenly the day became very important. The prospect during wartime of this day possibly being the last, re-presented the day as something to be embraced. The trick is to ensure it happens in peacetime. Norris continues: 'Now that we've gone back to worrying about what Ben Affleck eats for breakfast and what Jennifer Lopez is wearing, or not wearing, we might recall the seriousness to which we were called on September 11 and find something meaningful there.'[13] Life is a gift. The world was created *ex nihilo* (out of nothing), which all goes to say that I am not the centre of the world, God is. He is not dependent on me; rather I am dependent on him. Thus, life is something to be received gratefully. Each day is a gift. In the dying words of Georges Bernanos' sickly priest: 'Grace is . . . everywhere.'[14]

Passionate Living

How we enter into such a state of existence is, of course, a challenge. Short of a life-threatening illness, a major catastrophe like 9/11, or a major war, there are few opportunities available to us for developing such an intense, intentionally spiritual, way of living. Cultural self-sufficiency being what it is, there are few places left where we learn to receive life as a gift. The language of the market is so strong, even within the Christian community, that spiritual humility of the kind I am describing is regarded these days not so much as a virtue but as a weakness. One suspects it will take something like a 9/11 to make us see sense, since everything about our cultural education teaches us – from the womb it seems – to grab hold of life as a right. At the centre of all things is the notion of personal choice. And as long as this is the case, it is difficult to see how an essentially quiet humility towards life might emerge. As long as the goal of career growth is defined in terms of assertiveness, the beatitude of gratitude will always appear irrelevant.

However, as Robert Inchausti reminds us, there have always been, on the margins of the Christian world, holy fools who show us how to live well.[15] These revolutionaries warn us against the cult of big, and remind us that living a day well is unavoidably parochial; that a holy life is a celebration of the local and the immediate – an exploration into the fabric of one place, rather than, superficially, the souvenir shops of many places. In short, to live gratefully is to recognise that even if one never travelled beyond one's own backyard, it would still be possible to have lived well, for the truly prophetic life is lived out in actual places, with actual people, with actual stories. The setting is absolutely unique. And by entering into it, we see eternity in a day.

That we have lost our capacity for this kind of living is one of the more insidious effects of materialism. We have lost our sense of wonder. In Peter Shaffer's remarkable play, *Equus*, this theme is explored through the character of Dysart, the psychiatrist who is assigned to treat a deranged youth, sectioned for blinding six horses with a spike.[16] To be sure, the boy is deranged. His worship of the horse is indeed perverted. But after a time, Dysart begins to wonder who is insane. As he says to his friend:

I tell everyone that Margaret is the Puritan, I'm the pagan. Some pagan. Such wild returns I make to the womb of civilisation. Three weeks a year in the Peleponnese, every bed booked in advance, every meal paid for by vouchers, cautious jaunts in hired Fiats, suitcase crammed with Kao-Pectate. Such a fantastic surrender to the primitive. And I use that word endlessly: 'primitive.' 'Oh, the primitive world,' I say. 'What instinctual truths were lost with it!' And while I sit there, baiting a poor unimaginative woman with the word, that freaky boy tries to conjure the reality! I sit there looking at pages of centaurs, trampling the soil of Argos – and outside my window he is trying to become one, in a Hampshire field! . . . I watch that woman knitting night after night – a woman I haven't kissed in six years – and he stands in the dark for an hour, sucking the sweat off his God's hairy cheek! [Pause]. Then in the morning, I put away my books on the cultural shelf, close up the kodachrome snaps of Mount Olympus, touch my reproduction statue of Dionysus for luck – and go off to the hospital to treat him for insanity. Do you see?

Equus is one of the truly prophetic plays of our time. Set against the backdrop of meaningless, trivial existence, it offers to us a vision of an ordinary life lived passionately. In contrast to the passionless existence of Dysart and his wife, alleviated by 'three weeks a year in the Peleponnese', here is a young man who learns to embrace the particular, to find in one night in a Hampshire field more passion than Dysart has known in his life. Then, in the morning, while Dysart goes off to treat his patient for insanity, we, the audience, are left questioning whether it is we who are insane. For there is enough even in one day to fill our lives with wonder: taking the children to school, working at our desk, going out to the cinema, listening to music, washing the dishes, laughing with friends, making love – all of these are gifts.[17] We are meant to miss not one of them. To be forever rushing around, in simulated existence, inattentive to the great reservoirs of life contained in a single day, is madness itself, and what *Equus* is prophesying is that unless we recover our capacity for worship – at this most basic level of daily existence – we are ruined.

   In this respect, it is the monastics once again who witness most vividly to the immediacy of God's world and the sacramental possibilities of a day. For good or for ill, by inhabiting the confines of one place, the monastic life brings life down to its bare essentials. Without idealising the monastic way, it seems that within the walls of the monastery we have a chance to see a day for what it is. It confronts us. Stripped of media embellishment and deprived of the freedom to manoeuvre, the day emerges as the true entity it really is. This is the day, and there is no other. The testimony emerging from these overtly spiritual communities is just that: not so much an idealism about life in the cloister – most become disabused of that notion within a few days – but the utter uniqueness and particularity of each person and of each day.[18]

For me this love of place and day crystallises in the person of one of the brothers of a Benedictine community I visited once, near London. He and I were talking in the porch, waiting for the rain to stop, when I asked him how long he had lived in the community.

'Oh, let me see,' he replied. 'I joined here in 1958.'

What struck me immediately about his answer to my question was his complete indifference to how this might have sounded to someone like me. Indeed, when I asked him if he had ever considered moving to a different community I may as well have asked him if he had ever considered a summer holiday in Siberia. He looked bemused.

'Why would I want to do that? This is the community I joined. And this is where I will die.'

Thus, I was left with one unforgettable impression: of a culture passing through the seismic changes of the sixties revolution, the potential threat of nuclear war in the seventies, the unprecedented prosperity of right-wing Thatcherism in the eighties, and post-communist Europe in the nineties, and all this while he was there. To be sure, he was a school teacher, lest we imagine him in solitude all that time. Moreover, there is a strong case for saying that his staying in one place for such a long time was ill conceived. But that aside, what he bequeathed to me in that moment was an unquestionable passion for the local and for the daily. For him to have survived all those years, somewhere along the line he would have had to embrace the theological entity of a day, by more than just a casual acknowledgement, but as a matter of life and death. Which is of course precisely what happens in the monastery, as any visitor will tell you. Through the liturgy of the hours a day is embraced for all that it is worth.

Since mobility is so much a feature of modern living, it is hard to see how such a spirituality might develop. The freedom to move on, to move jobs, to change location, to change churches, is a basic inalienable right of the human constitution. It just wouldn't occur to most moderns that freedom of movement is inimical to the life of faith. On the contrary, to be a person of faith is, by definition, to be constantly seeking the next place, the next experience. However, we have within our Christian tradition a serious warning that this love of movement may often times not be a sign of faith, but of faithlessness; not so much an expression of enthusiasm but a fear of commitment; and not necessarily a love for God, but a spurning of people.

In fact, given that the heart of the Christian revelation is a celebration of the 'Christlike God', as Bishop John Taylor puts it, who enters into the messiness of our world, then the propensity of Christians to move from one place to another, in restless searching, is nothing less than spiritual apostasy. It is the abandonment of the ordinariness of incarnational living for the fantasy world of gnostic escapism. And people are turning over to it in droves, both outside the church and within. As Wendell Berry puts it in his short story *Pray without Ceasing*, which in its own way is a protest against modern wanderlust,

> And yet in Port William, as everywhere else, it was already the second decade of the twentieth century. And in some of the people of the town and the community surrounding it, one of the characteristic diseases of the twentieth century was making its way: the suspicion that they would be greatly improved if they were someplace else. This disease had entered into Thad Coulter and into Abner.[19]

However, as Berry relentlessly insists, the sacredness of life is never lived out in the abstract, someplace else, but in the actual here and now of this life, of this place, of this man and this woman. Christian spirituality is, after all, a celebration of the incarnation and therefore a move towards rather than away from the particular.

There are times, of course, when it is absolutely right to move on. But too often the desire to move on is precipitous – simply hurriedness – and a means of short-circuiting the formation that only living in one place, day after day, can teach us – which is where 'one day at a time' contracts are, again, hugely important. Instead of wishing one's life away in some fantasy future, with people who at last will understand us, living one day pays respect to the people who are here now. Instead of running off with our neighbour's wife, thinking that at last we have found our true soul mate, one day at a time forces us to confront the ordinariness of our own spouse, in the belief that the reality of this one wife is infinitely more glorious than the fantasy of a fictitious wife.[20] One-day contracts enable us to embrace life as it is. As Rowan Williams puts it: 'Here we are daily, not necessarily attractive and saintly people, managing the plain prose of our everyday service, deciding daily to recognise the prose of ourselves and each other as material for something unimaginably greater – the Kingdom of God, the glory of the saints, reconciliation and wonder.'[21]

Maybe this is what Luke intends by inserting that little word *daily* into his version of Christian discipleship. Whereas Mark records: 'If anyone would come after me he must deny himself and take up his cross and follow me,'[22] thus leaving us with the impression that Christian living could mean martyrdom, Luke interprets it as something far more mundane: 'If anyone would come after me, he must deny himself and take up his cross *daily* and follow me.'[23] Cross-bearing for Luke is not so much the grand gesture but daily fidelity to whatever God has put before us. Theologians say this is Luke's way of re-orientating discipleship to present day concerns as belief in the imminent return of Christ began to wane among the Christian community. Maybe so.[24] I prefer, however, to see it as Luke's way of ensuring that whatever we do believe about apocalyptic versions of the end of the world, or even apocalyptic visions of our own times, this should never be a substitute or a way of escaping the realities of daily commitments. Christian living is not so much being eaten by the lions; in one sense that would be easy. Rather, it is more like being trodden to death by a flock of geese. It is a slow and daily process. But through the ascesis of living daily, something deep emerges, rooted in the promise of the one who said 'For whoever wants to save his life will lose it, but whoever loses his life for me will save it.'[25]

'One day at a time' spirituality is hugely important, I believe, in a time of cultural ruination. It is not very sophisticated, I admit. But what it provides is a tool for survival. It delivers us from the anxieties of some mythical future and places us firmly into the particularity of what is before me in the here and now. In my last church we used to have an early morning prayer meeting and one dear brother used to pray out the same prayer every time we gathered: 'We cannot legislate for tomorrow, but we can live today. This is the day that the Lord has made, I will rejoice and be glad in it.'

3

Sabbath Rest

A Psalm for the Sabbath Day
It is good to praise the Lord
and make music to your name,
O most High,
to proclaim your love in the morning
and your faithfulness at night.[1]

Slaves cannot take a day off; free people can.[2]

I knew a rabbi once. He was the Principal of the High School where I worked in Israel as an English Assistant. He was also a chain-smoker. My recollection is that he smoked about sixty cigarettes a day. Wherever you saw him around the school, in the dining hall, in his office, in the playground, there he was with a cigarette. However, being a strict orthodox Jew he was presented with a dilemma when it came to observance of the most sacred day, for to light a fire on the Sabbath – in his tradition at least – was forbidden.

I guess he could have found a way around this problem if he wanted to – like the elevator to his flat, which worked on a Sabbath time switch; legalism has its own ways of circumventing the law. We call it hypocrisy. But surprisingly he didn't try. Neither did he break the law. On the contrary, on the Sabbath day he smoked not one cigarette. At least that is what he told me, and I had no reason to disbelieve him. His routine habit of sixty a day, Sunday to Friday, was temporarily suspended on the Saturday out of respect for the Law of Moses.

What was phenomenal, however – and the reason I tell the story – was the fact that he didn't even feel the need for a cigarette.

The Sabbath, he told me, was a day unlike any other day. On the Sabbath life entered into a whole different mode of existence, such that his compulsive addictions no longer gripped him the way they did the previous six days (and the way they surely would the following six days). Sabbath was time in suspension, and a foretaste of glory.

Perhaps this is not the best illustration with which to start a chapter on Sabbath. The story of my chain-smoking orthodox rabbi raises more questions than answers, not least that of the relationship between the Jewish Sabbath and the Christian Lord's Day. It also raises other questions relating to willpower. Why on earth, for instance, did he not harness some of that grace he experienced on the Sabbath for the other six days and kick the habit altogether? My guess, although I don't know this for certain, is that his habit eventually claimed his life. Even so – questions aside for a moment – for a young eighteen-year-old globetrotting on his gap year this chain-smoking rabbi was one of the Seven Wonders of the World; I have never forgotten him. And his story provokes us to think about Sabbath: to ask ourselves whether our own week has any kind of Sabbath rhythm to it. After all, how can you learn to live a day well, without to some degree being aware of the importance of this particular day which, in the history of religion, we call the Sabbath day? We may not be chain-smokers, but is our week properly punctuated with a six-day/one-day grammar?

Sabbath in the Bible

I perhaps ought to say at the outset that I am not a strict Sabbatarian – far from it. Even though the Olympian missionary Eric Liddell is one of my heroes, and *Chariots of Fire* one of my all-time favourite films,[3] I am not averse to running on the Sabbath, or even professional sport for that matter. My definition of Sabbath is closer to that described by Marva Dawn: that is, a day when you do something you really enjoy, when you 'do what you gladly choose to do'.[4] Although it is not a very precise definition and leaves a lot to the imagination, letting the imagination loose is precisely what Sabbath ought to be about. To argue the toss about whether one reads newspapers on a Sunday, or whether one plays football on a Sunday is, in my opinion, to miss the point of Sabbath, and to be guilty of the kind of theological nit-picking we see in the gospels concerning Sabbath observance. 'The Sabbath was made for man, not man for the Sabbath,'[5] said Jesus in response to an argument with the religious leaders of his day about the merits of picking grain on the Sabbath. It was a day when Jesus sought to liberate creation rather than tie it up in religious bondage.[6]

So I am not the best person to ask when it comes to the finer details of what to do on that day. But when it comes to actually taking a Sabbath I am very strict, as my colleagues will tell you. Based on the conviction that a pastoral life runs the risk of being every bit as secularised as any other job, and given that pastors' lives ought to act as something of a model to the congregations they serve, I insist that those of us who are called into the ministry of the church fully embrace the Sabbath. Jesus is, after all, Lord of the Sabbath.[7]

For a pastor of course that day is not a Sunday; at least in my tradition. But whatever day it is – and Paul seemed pretty relaxed about which day it was (Rom. 14:5) – my colleagues know that I am going to ask them whether they took it. And I can tell pretty much within two minutes whether they are telling me the truth or not. It is just like talking to an alcoholic. Even though technically they stopped work, the admission that they sneaked just a little tipple at the end of the day in some church meeting (that couldn't possibly be re-arranged) tells me that I am dealing with an inveterate workaholic. In fact, pastors are probably the worst offenders when it comes to breaking Sabbath. They are so busy being the Messiah that they cannot possibly see how the church would survive if they were to stop for one day. Some pastors pride themselves on the fact that they never take a day off. The work is too urgent, the demands too great to afford a rest. They are just too busy. If they do take a day off they take it not so much as a celebration of life so much as an anticipation of further work to come. The Sabbath is simply a means of recharging the batteries so that one can carry on with the work. A day off in this sense is not a Sabbath, but what Eugene Peterson calls a bastard Sabbath.[8]

Rather than shaping the week, a day off merely shadows the week, barely making a dent in our obsessive, task-driven lifestyle.

For a Sabbath to be truly a Sabbath one is thinking not simply about a day off, nor just stopping work – although in its most basic sense Sabbath means that.[9] Within the Judeo-Christian tradition we inhabit, Sabbath means a great deal more: to obey the fourth commandment is not only to desist but also to embrace; to enter into a different kind of day, whose repose gives meaning and energy to the other six days. Both the anticipation of the rest to come, and the aftermath of the rest enjoyed, inject proper rhythm into our lives, and ensure that life is not driven by the tyranny of the urgent but by the sovereignty of God. To not take a Sabbath is to vaunt oneself above God. It is to violate the *shalom* of God's creation. Ultimately it is an expression of deep ingratitude and rank infidelity, for it asserts the primacy of self over the graciousness of God. As Brueggemann puts it in his magisterial commentary on Genesis: 'The celebration of a day of rest was, then, the announcement of trust in this God who is confident enough to rest. It was then, as it is now, an assertion that life does not depend upon our feverish activity or self-securing; there can be a pause in which life is given to us simply as a gift.'[10]

A Protestant Play Ethic

In recognising the notion of gift inherent in the idea of Sabbath, it is no surprise that Martin Luther, the Protestant Reformer, harnessed the biblical doctrine of the Sabbath to his doctrine of justification by faith. Luther just couldn't help himself. He saw the doctrine of grace just about everywhere, often straining the plain meaning of the text to do so. But in this context he was right. In essence Sabbath is not just resting from our labour, but also from our efforts to justify ourselves by works: 'The spiritual rest which God especially intends in this commandment is that we not only cease from our labour and trade but much more – that we let God alone work in us and that in all our powers we do nothing of our own.'[11]

So important was the Sabbath in Jewish tradition that according to the rabbis 'it took a special act of creation to bring it into being, that the universe would be incomplete without it'.[12] Offensive as it may sound to those of us reared on a Protestant work ethic, the climax of the Genesis liturgy is not the creation of man and woman on the sixth day, but the blessing of the Sabbath on the seventh.[13] To be sure, because of the way the chapter breaks, it appears that the culmination of God's creative energy is the sixth day: the creation of men and women as co-workers with the Lord himself. Those who devised chapter and verse headings seem to have colluded in the human conspiracy to assert human work over play. But it is in fact the seventh day that is the pinnacle of the created order: 'And on the seventh day God rested from all his work. And God blessed the seventh day and made it holy, because on it he rested from all the work of creating he had done.'[14] In a world which is verging ever rapidly towards the idolatry of work and the mechanisation of culture, Sabbath represents the triumph of freedom over necessity, the celebration of play as the counterpart to work, and perhaps, most importantly, the recognition that the ultimate goal of our endeavours, not to mention the creation, is not technological advance, important though that is, but divine rest.[15]

Enacted properly, the Sabbath acts as a massive check on the awful utilitarianism of modern living, by reminding us once a week that we are not statistics in an impersonal system, but human beings made in the image of God. Quite apart from the issue of Sunday trading, a day of rest reminds us that we are not in essence consumers (probably the most hideous description yet of humankind) but persons in communion, whose hearts, as Augustine prayed to God, 'are restless until they find their rest in Thee'.[16] And although, as far as the world's agenda is concerned, a day of rest seems utterly useless, that is precisely the point: uselessness is what lies at the heart of the universe.[17] We are loved by God in Christ, not for what we do, but for who we are. You are my beloved.

Courting Death

There are issues, of course, surrounding our use of the Sabbath in this way, not least its relationship to the Christian Sunday, which we shall explore later. It is not immediately obvious how our Christian culture, let alone the wider culture, might recover the kind of rhythm described above. Nevertheless, quite apart from the practical issues of how one might go about re-instituting such a practice, the purpose of the above discussion is to underline that there is something radically on offer with the construction of the week around a Sabbath rest, akin to the redemption of time we described earlier.

To embrace the Sabbath is to enter a different construct of time that transcends chronological time even as it remains wedded to it. It is to live liturgically instead of randomly and thus create a cathedral space in the midst of city chaos; or, to change the metaphor, an oasis in the middle of the desert. As Abraham Heschel notes in what must be the definitive treatise on the Jewish Sabbath, the creation of the Sabbath 'is a radical departure from accustomed religious thinking. The mythical mind would expect that, after heaven and earth have been established, God would create a holy place – a holy mountain or a holy spring – whereupon a sanctuary is to be established. Yet it seems as if to the Bible it is *holiness in time*, the Sabbath, which comes first.'[18] If modern living is man's conquest of space at the expense of time, then keeping Sabbath is the redemption of time, and the victory of time over space. Those who keep the Sabbath effectively sanctify time and protect the human soul from the corrosion of a purely technological approach.

I like what Mark Buchanan says, in this respect, about the violation of the Sabbath as it appears in Numbers (which, as he says, is about the only story in all Scripture that gives any real indication of the kind of activity God forbids on the Sabbath). Commenting on the man found gathering wood on the Sabbath day, and the subsequent decision by the assembly to have the man stoned to death, Buchanan notes that 'the punishment seems grossly out of proportion to the crime'.[19] Indeed it does. Had the offence been adultery we might have understood. To stone someone for adultery at least sounds Old Testament, but to stone someone to death for breaking the Sabbath because he was gathering wood sounds a bit extreme. What kind of justice is that?

However, as Buchanan wryly notes about the anxious lifestyle of the man gathering wood: 'Such living always carries with it a death penalty.' Persons who refuse to stop work are already, in many ways, courting a culture of death. They are consistently violating the creation liturgy with some makeshift liturgy of their own, so contrary to the way the world has been set up that, in the end, it de-humanises. We know this from the way the command to keep the Sabbath is reframed in Deuteronomy on the eve of crossing into the Promised Land: 'Remember that you were slaves in Egypt and that the Lord your God brought you out of there with a mighty hand and an outstretched arm. Therefore the Lord your God has commanded you to observe the Sabbath day.'[20] Hence, the Israelites are to keep the Sabbath, not simply because God rested from his labour, which is the ostensible reason given in Exodus 19:11, but also because to renege on the Sabbath is to return to a world of slavery, a world without pause. It is to forget one's baptismal identity as an adopted son, in which people are named and loved, and to prefer instead the slavery of Egypt where numbers and quotas rule the day. For sure, such a regime has its own enticements. There is a long history of the people of God dreaming of the fleshpots of Egypt. But in the end it is a road to death. Sabbath keeps us, even as we keep the Sabbath, from this kind of reductionism, and transfers us into bigger country and a larger space where instead of suffocating under the burden of serious living, at last we can breathe the fresh air of a baptised, God-centred life.

Of course, what constitutes Sabbath-breaking in the present context varies from person to person. Since we are not insisting on a strict nor overtly religious definition of Sabbath keeping, it follows that enjoying the Sabbath for one person could constitute violating the Sabbath for another. I am not about to devise a list of prohibitions, nor a series of prescriptions for that matter (although who would protest against Bass' advice that 'it is a good deed for married couples to have sexual intercourse on Shabbat'?).[21] However, to observe Sabbath well, and, more importantly, in order to inject a Sabbath rhythm into the whole of the week, it seems to me that one has to become scrupulously honest about the kind of activities that disturb one's rest, and the kind of activities that promote it. For instance, wood gathering in our own context may constitute rest; checking our e-mails, however, may involve us courting death. Indeed, given the ubiquitous

nature of e-mail and the way so many of us complain of its tyranny, it may well be that avoiding e-mail for a day (or even
avoiding it altogether), is really all that is needed for some
people in order to demarcate a Sabbath. If I can resist looking at
my e-mails for a day, I know I have a pretty good chance of entering into a different frame of mind. In fact, a friend of mine went
further than this. He sent a circular to all his friends in which he
announced that he was officially leaving the world of e-mail. If
we wanted to contact him, he said, we would have to write a
decent letter or make a phone call. This courageous act was not
just about preserving one day of rest; it was about injecting rest
into the whole of our week. And although I have not followed
suit, and still from time to time wreck a day off by checking my
e-mails, I kind of like the idea that someone out there has had the
guts to take off the noose and try to start breathing again.

As I say, it is not for me to prescribe. I am not especially inter-
ested in the mechanics of Sabbath, more the rhythm of it.
Furthermore, my interest lies beyond just one day. My point is
that by taking a day of rest that same Sabbath repose might recur
in other places throughout the week. Indeed, it could be argued
that the New Testament vision is that every day is a Sabbath day
– every day an attempt to enter God's rest. Again, it has nothing
to do with passivity – that way lies laziness. It has everything to
do with trust. Every day becomes a choice over whether I trust
God or my own ingenuity. But keeping Sabbath is a good place to
start (just as tithing might be a good place to start for those wanting to give). By doing nothing for one day, we serve notice on the
powers that be that we belong to another kingdom. By sitting
down, we remind ourselves that oftentimes what we don't do is
as important, if not more important, than what we do do.

It takes a lot of guts, to be sure. To not study for one day, whilst
everyone else is cramming for finals at the college library, requires
a lot of faith; to forgo the latest DIY project, and play instead with
the children, is tantamount to a Damascus road conversion; to
avoid the shopping mall and to go walking instead in the countryside is like Peter walking on water: it is a scary business. How
on earth will we survive? Yet, strangely enough, we do survive.
The shops don't go away, and the house still stands. Furthermore,
those who play hard, as well as work hard, are often top in the

end-of-year exams. It is a proven fact that workaholism, like all addictions, backfires on itself. A restless mind is good for nothing. So, far from hindering our prospects, Sabbath sets them up. It sets the pace for the rest of the week. It reminds us that God can be trusted with our lives. We are not so important that we cannot stop. At the end of the day, so to speak, we are the created not the Creator. If I don't do it, the world will still go around. Meanwhile, I have a task on my hands, one which requires all my effort: the task of entering his rest.

A Church at Ease with Itself

The power of the Sabbath to act in such liberating ways perhaps seems rather over-inflated, not least because there is a deep nervousness, among Protestants in particular, that churchly disciplines like these are simply an expression of works righteousness, or religious exclusivity and therefore a threat to the gospel of grace. I have some sympathy with this. There is a sense in which during the exile the Sabbath became too important as a cultural badge, which is why Jesus spoke against it, and Paul sought to relativise it. Membership of the people of God is not on the basis of religious identity markers, but by grace through faith.[22] But to relativise something is not to totally dismiss it. Sabbath has, at other times, played an important role in fostering vitality, as Achad Hamm observes in the history of the Jews in the Diaspora: 'If the Sabbath had not restored to them the soul, renewing every week their spiritual life, they would have become so degraded by the depressing experiences of the workdays, that they would have descended to the last steps of materialism and of moral and intellectual decadence.'[23]

In short, grace thrives on habitual response; more specifically, keeping the Sabbath regulates freedom. Without the practice of Sabbath keeping, grace lacks proper footholds, in the same way that love without the practice of hospitality is just words. It is a misunderstanding of life in the Spirit to suppose that it requires no discipline. Discipline is to spiritual formation what learning scales is to piano playing. How can one play grace notes without that underlying musical structure? And unless we recover these churchly practices, Western Christianity will be in danger of the same moral decline as that described by Hamm. Indeed, I would put it more strongly: unless contemporary models of church life overthrow this Protestant nervousness about discipline, and become far more intentional about the relationship between the celebration of discipline and spiritual formation, one fears that Christian communities will themselves succumb to the distractedness that is now so blatant in our own times.[24] The restoration of the Sabbath day is critical to the reassertion of Christian faith.

It is worth noting at this point that the practice of Sabbath keeping, whatever form it might take, is quite different from the practice of Lord's Day worship. Since for the early Christians the Lord's Day was a working day, it doesn't take much to work out that Sunday as a day of rest was instituted later on the back of the Christendom enterprise.[25] So I am not for one minute suggesting that worship and rest are synonymous. It may well be that Sunday takes on that particular characteristic for some; for others it has too many religious connotations to be helpful. Indeed I hope it has become clear that this chapter is not a plea for a strict Sabbath, nor even a Sabbath day once a week, but rather some semblance of a Sabbath rhythm where work is punctuated by frequent rest. And this, not in order to legitimise our work but rather to explore a different way of being human altogether: one in which playfulness supersedes utilitarianism.

Judging by the faces of the people I see Sunday by Sunday, however, we are not doing too well at this. I doubt whether many in our congregations have the first idea about what it means to truly rest. Furthermore churches are often complicit in the crime. Rather than offering the world a window onto a different way of living, acting as the vanguards of a new creation, churches themselves can simply mimic the busyness of the world, ending up with what can only be described as congregational tiredness. If a Sabbath-keeping, Jesus-centred people are supposed to announce a Jubilee to the world, in which debts get cancelled and the land is replenished,[26] then what churches often announce instead is an ill-conceived programme by which real Christian formation is sacrificed on the altar of church activity.

Maybe this criticism is too strong. Every church requires a programme of sorts; and every pastor needs to be able to run the church. The problems start when the programme *becomes* the church and when the running of the church *becomes* the pastoral vocation. One of the ways to arrest this descent is for the pastor to keep Sabbath. If violating the Sabbath is a sure indicator that things are not well, that I am taking myself too seriously; conversely, taking the Sabbath checks my latent messianism, confirming to me that the world and – perhaps more importantly – the church can survive without me.

Indeed, I would say that Sabbath has been as critical to my work as just about any other spiritual discipline; so much so that my advice to other men and women entering the pastorate is to, above all else, keep Sabbath. If you keep Sabbath I guarantee you a long and fruitful ministry; if you don't keep Sabbath you can expect nothing more than disaster. It is as simple as that. Yes there are strategies to employ, leadership conferences to attend, books to read, and programmes to enact; but strangely enough the greatest leadership gift pastors can bequeath to their congregations is the lost art of stopping. Over and above what we pastors get our congregations to do by way of activities is what we get our congregations not to do, for congregations also need a Sabbath rest.[27]

Without Sabbath, Christian communities degenerate into 'doing church' rather than 'being church' – an easier option no doubt, since we are well trained in the art of doing. And although there is something to be said for Christian activism, this is far short of what a Christian community can be. Churches are not recruiting agencies, nor merely centres of activity. They are not a means to an end. Rather, the church exists to be itself. Churches that consciously enter into a Sabbath rhythm, both in terms of the pattern of its ministry as well as the shape of its programme, protect this being of the church, and hopefully model to the world an alternative way of human community. Without Sabbath we lose hope. Christian community ends up as bland as the world it has come from; with Sabbath, the church becomes a foretaste of the eschatological future of God.

Postscript

For anyone wanting to venture into the unknown world of Sabbath-keeping my advice would be to first read Heschel's classic, *The Sabbath*. I have quoted it a few times in this chapter already, but could have done so far more extensively. He is eminently quotable. How about this for an opening salvo: 'Six days a week we wrestle with the world, wringing profit from the earth; on the Sabbath we especially care for the seed of eternity planted in the soul.'[28] We need not deduce from this some ethereal mysticism, or anti-modernism. As Heschel notes later on, 'The solution of mankind's most vexing problems will not be found in renouncing technical civilisation, but in attaining some degree of independence from it.'[29] He was a twentieth-century man, after all.

What startled me however, purchasing my own hardbound copy of *The Sabbath* only recently, is his recounting of a well-known Jewish tale concerning a rabbi who was immured by his persecutors in a cave, 'so that he knew not when it was day or night'. Consequently, he was not able to discern the passing of each day, and more specifically the Sabbath day, presaged by the dimming light of a Friday evening. He was grief-stricken. His grief at not being able to celebrate the Sabbath was further compounded by his inability to conquer his passion for smoking. In so many ways he was a poor Jew.

However, like my rabbi friend all those years ago, the one thing about the Sabbath was that this imprisoned Jew's desire for smoking completely left him. For some inexplicable reason on the Sabbath he was free of his addiction. And in this strange phenomenon the story finds a wonderful and surprising resolution, for 'All at once,' Heschel recounts, the rabbi perceived that his desire to smoke suddenly vanished and a voice said within him: 'Now it is Friday evening! For this was always the hour when my longing for that which is forbidden on the Sabbath regularly left me.'[30] Thus it continued from week to week: 'his tormenting desire for tobacco regularly vanished at the incoming of each Sabbath.'[31]

After all these years I now wonder whether my rabbi friend was telling me his own story or simply recounting to me this well-known Jewish tale. Twenty-five years on I am unlikely to find out. Either way, I will never forget him, nor the lesson he passed on to me: that a truly free life must include within it the courage to Sabbath. As Wendell Berry expresses in one of his poems:

Whatever is foreseen in joy
Must be lived out from day to day.
Vision held open in the dark
By our ten thousand days of work.
Harvest will fill the barn; for that
The hand must ache, the face must sweat.
And yet no leaf or grain is filled
By work of ours; the field is tilled
And left to grace. That we may reap,
Great work is done while we're asleep.
When we work well, a Sabbath mood
Rests on our day, and finds it good.[32]

INTERLUDE

A Sermon on Naboth's Vineyard

All theology is preached theology, or should be. Theology is not the preserve of the academy but the church. The pulpit rather than the lectern is where all good theology ought to begin.[1]

I preached this sermon long before I started writing the book, but when I look back I can see that so many of the ideas found in this book were there in seedling form in the sermon. So it is that writing a sermon, for me at least, is a prelude to writing a book, and writing a book is a preparation for preaching a sermon; they are one and the same.

I offer this sermon in the hope that through the very different medium of the pulpit, some of the themes I have sought to elucidate in the book are clarified, this first part in particular. Although the printed sermon is something of a contradiction in terms, even in print I think it retains its somewhat different mood. And, what it preaches is a popular version of the same burden found in the book: namely a deep sadness about a culture of commodification, and a prophetic longing to recover the simplicity of biblical faith.

For some readers such a take may be an illegitimate reading of the ancient text: a classic case of reading contemporary concerns into the Old Testament; or, to use preaching parlance, a severe case of eisegesis rather than exegesis. But I don't think so. It is Brueggemann who shows us not only the homiletical fun a preacher and congregation can have in a few well-chosen anachronisms (such as my Elijah cancelling his Saga holiday in order to confront Jezebel), but also the hermeneutical legitimacy of seeing the ideological conflict between the royal court and the prophetic circle as the modern conflict between commodity theory and distributional theory.[2] Brueggemann's language, one has to admit, is sometimes overly socio-economic; and there are times when for all the world he reads like a Marxist. The way Brueggemann sets royal ideology over against Yahwistic faith is, in my opinion, sometimes overdone and fails to take account of the way even Jesus, for instance, models himself on the royal court – 'one greater than Solomon'. That said, I have consistently found Brueggemann to be a wonderful help for closing the gap between the two horizons that exist for every preacher: namely the biblical text and the contemporary world. In an almost imperceptible way he convinces the reader that the pitched battles between the royal court and the prophetic school are indeed archetypical conflicts between two ways of living: the conflict between the House of Ahab and Naboth the Jezreelite is a modern day parable of the conflict between the consumer world of big corporations in which everything seems to be commodified, and the actual world of local, parochial communities in which the community is valued simply for itself.

As I have sought to explain, this is not the age-old stand off between industrial and rural communities; nor is it an attack on technology *per se*. There is much that is good about technological advance. What this sermon does attack, however, is the way in which the hubris that inevitably accompanies technological advance has had a terrible way of trivialising, if not destroying, the soul. Hence, it is significant that the underdog in the narrative is accorded the dignity of a name and a history: Naboth the Jezreelite. Furthermore, I have made much of the fact that he owned a vineyard and that Ahab wanted to return it to being a vegetable plot. The idea is not original (I took it from a footnote in Iain Provan's fine commentary on 1 and 2 Kings),[3] nor is it entirely convincing, but with a bit of preacher's licence I have taken the intention to replace a vineyard with a vegetable plot as symbolic of something that is most definitely attacked in the narrative: namely the self-reliance of the powerful over and against the humility of trust that God requires of his people. And if this means that we act to some degree as critics of the impersonal, rapacious nature of the McWorld, then so be it. In my opinion, we are in good company.

The Sermon: 1 Kings 21

What do Frank Sinatra, Zinedine Zidane, and Elijah the Tishbite have in common?
Blue eyes? All kicked with their left foot? No. They all came out of retirement in response to the need of the hour – in Zidane's case to help an ailing football team; in Sinatra's case more times than anyone can now remember; in Elijah's case, after having languished a few years, a comeback in response to a show trial up over in the Jezreel valley, where Naboth, a small landholder, had been stoned to death by the townsfolk for allegedly blaspheming the Lord. Everyone knew that the real reason was because he had refused to sell his vineyard to the royal palace.

But of course the first question that strikes you in the story is this: knowing how godless and idolatrous the king and queen were, why didn't Naboth sell in the first place? After all, his land did border the perimeter of the king's grounds. He could see the wall every time he walked his vineyard to check the grapes; and, to be fair to Ahab, the king had made a reasonable offer of money, as well as an offer to relocate the family plot. Why be such a stick in the mud? Why so stubborn? Knowing full well that even though Ahab at worst might sulk and throw his toys out of the pram, Jezebel, his wife, (who must surely be the original neighbour from hell), would not take no for an answer, and set up some contract killing. Wouldn't it have been easier to just cave in and up sticks?

And the answer, once you have trawled the commentaries and done a bit of ancient history, is this: that it is better to die than to sell out to the world of big corporations; better to be falsely accused and stoned to death than to suffer the judgement of God for faithlessness.

Let me explain. Land in ancient Israel, as we have seen in the Gaza strip in recent years in modern Israel, is not just a piece of dirt that you can speculate on. As far as an Israelite was concerned it was a gift from the Lord, an inheritance. When they entered the land, driving out the previous inhabitants, Joshua allocated it to the tribes as their inheritance. Therefore it was not open to individuals to sell land in perpetuity. What is more, laws were in place to prevent precisely this kind of thing happening:

namely, the accumulation of wealth in the hands of a few, even if it was the king. For, whatever else Israel was, it was a nation that was called to demonstrate God's justice, his love for the poor.

But, the fact that Ahab desires to make a vegetable plot (*gan yaraq*) out of Naboth's vineyard once he has purchased it is also significant, and may account for Naboth's refusal. As it says in Deuteronomy 11:10, it is exactly this predictable and man-made way of cultivation that Israel had to give up when she left Egypt, in preference for a land – a vineyard in fact – that relied upon God for its health. Let me read to you from Deuteronomy:

> The land you are entering to take over is not like the land of Egypt, from which you have come, where you planted your seed and irrigated it by foot as in a vegetable garden. But the land you are crossing to take possession of is a land of mountains and valleys that drinks rain from heaven. It is a land the Lord your God cares for, the eyes of the Lord are continually on it from the beginning of the year until its end.'

In fact, I would say, purely from a geographical point of view, that is precisely why God called them to his part of the world, a piece of land no bigger than Wales: because it wasn't predictable, like the Nile through Egypt. And so right at the outset she had to rely on God, stay faithful (vv. 13–15).

So this is no innocent request from Ahab for a neighbour's vineyard, no attempt to grow some prize leeks and cucumbers for the Jezreel summer fête. No. This is the habit of a lifetime, every bit as wicked as employing the prophets of Baal in his court: a sinister attempt to go back to Egypt, to go it alone, to treat the gift as an acquisition, and to rape faithful Israelites of their family inheritance so that the king might have more and more power. It is the replacement of trust, fidelity and prayer, which is how we are to receive life, with possessiveness; it is the destruction of community, local history, of named individuals, by impersonal power and might; it is the violation of the land and its blessing by property speculation; the replacement of grace and thanksgiving by a world in which everything is viewed as a commodity. And the reason we don't notice how offensive it was to

Naboth, and why he didn't sell, is because that is also how we have been trained to see the world: as a gallery of commodities.

And so off we go to Disney World (and I have nothing against Disney) and queue for an hour so we can go round a simulated lake, when we could just as easily go down to the river here, and see kingfishers and deer, and catch crayfish, all for the cost of a rowing boat. Or we crowd into McDonald's, get our meal deals, have endless TV dinners, watch 17,000 adverts a year, and go for months without a decent meal around the table, because we prefer to live life vicariously.

But you see, whilst we might treat life as a commodity – as a thing to possess, pick up and throw away – and people like Naboth, and his little vineyard, as dispensable – God doesn't. Naboth was precious to him, along with the many other small landholders like him. Whilst Ahab saw land to speculate on, God saw not grapes as such, but a family, a tradition, and an inheritance; the forebears of Naboth, his sons, his daughters, his wife, his friends; his thankfulness; his lighting of the Sabbath candles at the end of the week; the laughter around the table when his friends would come over; his thankfulness to God for the harvest; his prayers to God for rain, without which there would be no harvest; his hospitality to strangers, outsiders, the poor; his time. Like Dorothy Hartley said, in describing our technological world: 'A modern woman sees a piece of linen, but the woman of the past saw through it to the flax fields, she smelt the reek of the retting ponds, she felt the hard rasp of the rackling and she saw the soft sheen of the glossy flax.' God saw all this and he loved it. (Why do you think we have bread and wine to celebrate the death of our Lord Jesus?) And above all, he loved Naboth's zeal to preserve it from the lustful eyes of a greedy, idolatrous king, even though Naboth knew it would cost him his life – which it did.

Although Ahab simply sulked, which is what he always did (see 1 Kings 20, where the Lord ticks him off for not putting an end to Ben-Hadad) when he couldn't get his way (as my mother used to say, 'He's having a do'), Jezebel took matters into her own hands and arranged a religious ceremony in order to stone him. And seeing all this, how a person can use even a solemn fast as a cloak for murder, the Lord God wakes his favourite prophet from retirement, tells him to put away his Saga magazine for a moment, and get back on the road. Because whatever else we want to say about our God – and there is a lot we want to say about our God – he is zealous for his people. Whilst we live in a world where we notice the ninety-nine, God looks after the one: Naboth, the Jezreelite, who owned a vineyard near the king's palace.

I am sure Ahab was thrilled when he saw Elijah striding towards him down one of the rows of his newly acquired vineyard. Is there nowhere that I can hide? He thought Elijah was on some Mediterranean cruise. I should think his heart sank. And not being one to disappoint, Elijah the Tishbite delivers one of his best sermon lines yet: 'So you are a cut-throat as well as a con man!' Because, of course, as the ten commandments teach us, once you break the first commandment – that you shall have no other gods before me (Ahab had done that) – then what follows is a whole litany of sins: covetousness, false testimony, murder, and theft, all in one chapter. And then all this stuff about dogs: dogs licking up Ahab's blood instead of Naboth's, dogs devouring Jezebel by the wall of Jezreel. Justice delayed is not justice denied. God sees everything – and what God's prophet delivers is not just comfort for the afflicted but affliction for the comfortable.

But what is fascinating to me is that right at the end it says that Ahab – as far gone as he was – tore his clothes, put on sackcloth, fasted and went around humbly. Isn't that amazing? At this eleventh hour he sees the light, and God responds to it: 'I will not bring disaster in his day, but on the house of his son.' Which, believe you me, was a mercy. And it is as if God is saying there is almost no place you can go that the grace of God, the word of God cannot reach you, if you humble yourself. You can be a rank idolater, a liar and a cheat but if you humble yourself there is still hope.

PART TWO:

THE LITURGY OF THE HOURS

Prologue to Part Two

I call to God,
And the Lord saves me.
Evening, morning and noon
I cry out in distress
And he hears my voice.[1]

I have long been fascinated by monastic communities. Part of me rejects the idea of a select group of men separated from the world by the cloister. On the other hand, part of me is captivated by the kind of prayerful rhythms the life of a monk affords. In a world that has lost all sense of reverence, living liturgically according to the prayerful contours of the monastic hours has a lot to be said for it, since it gets us to pay attention to the different moods of the day, praying through each one of them and thus sanctifying the day.

In Part Two I therefore want to offer a tripartite rhythm of prayer that distils some of the wisdom of the monastery to ordinary lay people like us. Clearly we can't embrace all the hours. For good reason, changes were put in place many centuries ago that transposed the keys of the monastery to what was referred to as the cathedral worship of the people of God in the real world; furthermore, by focusing on the rudimentary hours of morning, noon and evening, I hope to keep us practical as well as mystical. Praying through the various hours or moods of the day is not the preserve of the monk, but basic Christianity, for all who seek to follow Christ. Nevertheless, what I hope to prove is that prayerful rhythm, of the kind we might find in the monastery, is pivotal to the call to live one day at a time.

4

Your Mercies are New Every Morning

And though the last lights off the black West went
Oh, morning, at the brown brink eastward, springs –
Because the Holy Ghost over the bent
World broods with warm breast and with ah! bright wings.[1]

Most people are either a lark or an owl. Some people like to rise early; others like going to bed late. For sure, there are people who can do both; those who burn the candle at both ends. Maybe they are the people the Psalmist describes when he says 'in vain they rise early and stay up late'.[2] But generally you are either one or the other. For instance, a friend of mine begins his best work, he tells me, at ten o'clock every night, invariably staying up until one or two in the morning. Others of us turn into pumpkins after eleven, yet delight in the peace and quiet of the early morning hours. Whichever you are – a lark or an owl – my hope is that you will find something in this chapter to inspire you. After all, everyone has to get up at some time or other. And in order for the day to be *yours*, to quote the title of the book, how we approach the morning is critical for a life of faith. A day can be won or lost in the first hour of the morning.

Over the years I have wondered if one of the reasons for my own liking of the early morning is a perverse joy in thinking that one has got a head start. During my college years I was guilty of a certain Pharisaical smugness, no doubt, about rising early when so many of my fellow students were only just hitting the sack, weary from the night's drinking. Over the years, however, I have come to realise that my love for rising early is not attributable to that at all; rather, the morning, or even the early morning, while it is still dark, offers the promise of encounter.

Such a claim, I am sure, has already ostracised a good many of those reading this chapter. For those who struggle to get out of bed in the morning there is nothing worse, as Proverbs says, than the cheerfulness of an early riser: 'If a man loudly blesses his neighbour early in the morning, it will be taken as a curse.'[3] Such proverbial wisdom suggests, moreover, that there is nothing particularly spiritual or meritorious about getting up early. My wife Susanna, for instance, though a disciplined and prayerful person, has never found early mornings easy, and it is not something that she should feel condemned for. If the body needs so many hours of sleep, that's just the way it is. It has very little to do with spirituality, in the first instance. My contention, however, is that morning prayer holds out to us a special kind of seduction. As morning light wrestles with the darkness, and overcomes yet again the mysterious blackness that precedes the day, so the dawn also brings us word of a love that is just as conquering and faithful; an ordained rotation of the earth's axis, the routine of night passing into day, opens up an unmerited, unexplained surprise that 'This is the day that the Lord has made, let us rejoice and be glad in it.'[4]

Resurrection Morning

Significantly, rising early to seek God was a practice of Jesus himself. 'Very early in the morning, while it was still dark, Jesus got up, left the house, and went off to a solitary place, where he prayed.'[5] As Jesus was steeped in the Psalms this practice really ought to come as no surprise: the Psalmist reckons early morning to be the time when God bears witness to his love.[6] If the evening is time to reflect on his faithfulness, then the morning is a time to celebrate the freshness of his love. 'Let the morning bring me word of your unfailing love,' pleads the Psalmist,[7] echoing the proclamation that 'weeping may linger for the night, but joy comes with the morning'.[8] Indeed, by the time we reach the prophets there is a veritable tradition emerging of early morning rising. Just as a traveller would set off early in the morning to attend to urgent business, so the prophet wakes early to hear the word of the Lord.[9] To quote one of our own proverbs: 'the early bird catches the worm'. So whilst it would be harmful to make a virtue or a legalism out of this, equally it would be wrong to dismiss the significance of the early morning altogether as a time of spiritual receptivity. A businessman knows how important discipline is if he wants to make an early start; he has his own liturgy of the hours. All we are saying is that the Bible points to a similar discipline for those who call themselves Christian.

A major advocate of early morning prayer is the German theologian Bonhoeffer – a Christian who did so much, of course, to keep Christian faith alive when the German church showed every sign of capitulating to Nazi ideology in the 1930s. In a sustained piece of theological reflection for the benefit of the students of Finkenwalde, Bonhoeffer expounds on the importance of morning prayer, linking it to the very heart of the Christian gospel. Night passing into morning is, for Bonhoeffer, nothing less than a reflex of the death and resurrection of Christ. 'At night Christ was born, a light in the darkness; noonday turned to night when Christ suffered and died on the Cross. But in the dawn of the Easter morning Christ rose in victory from the grave.'[10] Hence, 'At the break of light it remembers the morning on which death and sin lay prostrate in defeat and new life and salvation were given to mankind.'[11]

This framing of the gospel story in images of morning light and evening darkness is nothing that John doesn't claim at the end of his gospel. The resurrection of Jesus, as we shall explore in more depth when we look at Lord's Day worship, is framed in the context of night and day, light and darkness. Just as the Lord God searched for Adam in the garden in the cool of the evening, and found him wanting, so Mary encounters the gardener in the early morning light and discovers him to be the risen Lord. And there is no doubt that John – no less than Luke – intends us to read this in terms of Sunday worship, for it was 'early on the first day of the week'.[12] But, in a sense, every day, as Bonhoeffer seeks to persuade us, takes on this particular twist. Every new day is a resurrection announcement. As Lancelot Andrewes puts it in his famous *Private Devotions*:

Blessed are Thou, O Lord,
Our God,
The God of our fathers;
Who turnest the shadow of death into the morning,
And renewest the face of the earth;
Who rollest away the darkness before the light,
banishest night, and bringest back the day;
Who lightenest my eyes,
Lest I sleep the sleep of death;
Who deliverest me from the terror of the night,
From the pestilence that walketh in the darkness;
Who drivest sleep from mine eyes,
And slumber from mine eyelids;
Who makest the outgoings of the morning and the evening to rejoice.[13]

Andrewes fashioned his *Private Devotions* around the seven days of creation. As Alexander Whyte puts it in his interpretation of the devotions: 'The First chapter of Genesis supplies to Andrewes the mould and the framework upon which he shapes and constructs his book, and a right noble use he makes of the majestic movement and the splendid scenery of that superb chapter.'[14] It is no surprise that morning prayer features throughout, including additional prayers 'on awakening'. Rooted in the very first day of creation, when God said 'Let there be Light,' we pray with Andrewes: 'By thy resurrection raise us up unto newness of life, supplying to us frames of repentance.'[15]

One of the difficulties we have in appropriating this liturgical take on the early morning is that night-time no longer holds the terror that it once did in pre-modern societies – a point alluded to by Bonhoeffer himself at some point in the discussion of early morning prayer. Rather like the way grace can only be understood in the context of judgement, so resurrection light can only be fully appreciated against the backdrop of midnight darkness. As A. Roger Ekirch points out in his fascinating study of the history of night-time prior to 1830, the hours of darkness were regarded with such fear by many that even some writers like the otherwise quite rational Anglican bishop Jeremy Taylor believed that night was the special dominion of the devil, supposing 'that God had forbidden his presence during daytime'.[16]

Ekirch shows that prior to the invention of the electric light bulb, the nocturnal world was fairly replete, in the popular psyche at least, with noxious vapours, screeching animals and demonic spirits.[17] Thank God for Edison! But if the terror of the night-time has all but been demystified, as well as demythologised, then what chance does this kind of liturgical spirituality have? Without some fear of the night, the morning ceases to be anything at all. In fact, as I mentioned in the introduction, in some societies now there is no passing into night at all. Consequently, the morning no longer heralds anything, save a few on-the-hour news bulletins. This is not an argument to say we ought to go back to candlelight, but rather that somewhere we need to rediscover the joy the Psalmist experienced with the arrival of the dawn light. Scripture after scripture, Bonhoeffer reminds us,

> tells us that the first thought and the first word of the day belong to God; 'My voice shalt thou hear in the morning, O Lord. In the morning will I direct my prayer unto thee' (Ps. 5:3). 'My heart is fixed, O God, my heart is fixed: I will sing and give praise. Awake up, my glory; awake, psaltery and harp: I myself will awake early' (Ps. 57:7, 8). At the dawn of day the believer thirsts and yearns for God: I prevented the dawning of the morning, and cried: I hope in thy word' (Ps. 119:147). 'O God, thou art my God, early will I seek thee; my soul thirsteth for thee, my flesh longeth for thee in a dry and thirsty land, where no water is' (Ps. 63:1).

Bonhoeffer concludes with references from the Wisdom of Solomon and Ecclesiasticus, claiming also with Psalm 46:5 and Lamentations 3:23, that the morning hour 'is the time of God's special help'.[18] To be sure, 'some rise early because of restlessness and worry,' notes Bonhoeffer, 'but there is such a thing as rising early for the love of God'.[19] Moreover, given the silence of night and early morning, 'hymns and the Word of God are more easily grasped'.[20]

Your Mercies are New Every Morning

Again, I am not so sure these days how many will agree with this last statement. At seven in the morning it is a wonder anything is grasped, let alone hymns and the word of God; maybe a comb or a cup of coffee, but definitely not the word of God and prayer. But I reckon the experience, described by the writer of Lamentations, of receiving a love that is as regular and as faithful as a new morning, is well nigh universal among believers. Speaking from the vantage point of the pastorate (a vantage point that we pastors ought to make more of, in my opinion, when it comes to writing theology), I come across many Christians who know exactly what Lamentations 3:23 refers to, for without the punctuation of night passing into day the accumulation of anxiety, doubt, fear, guilt, bitterness, and jealousy would indeed consume us. Like the people of God in Jeremiah's day, following the destruction of Jerusalem, life would be one long alphabet of judgement and guilt. But God's love is like the morning. At the very least, the regular repetition of the morning breaks up anxiety into manageable proportions; more than that, it signals God's commitment to renew his grace over our lives. Set against the backdrop of the night, which is the only backdrop for understanding Christian spirituality (lest it descends into a kind of sentimentality), the creeping light of the morning hours heralds the possibility of grace. 'The chaos and darkness of suffering become the first-day light.'[21] Like a good sermon illustration, the conquest of light over darkness one more time illuminates the triumph of God's mercies over his judgement. And but for this we would be utterly consumed.

This is why the early morning is so important for us. Morning is like the tide coming in, washing over the debris of half-finished lives and presenting once again, for this day at least, new opportunities for holiness. It is a kind of sacrament – a means of grace, if you will – and like all means of grace, it really does deliver what it promises. Simply entering a new day prayerlessly, therefore, inattentive to the particular movement of God's grace that is invested in the turning of the earth's axis, is to live distractedly. 'The early morning belongs to the Church of the Risen Christ.'[22]

Those who are devotees of Bonhoeffer's biography know that many of his students balked at his rigorism concerning morning prayer at the quasi-monastic community in Finkenwalde. His point, however, was not that the disciplines of prayer are a precondition of God's grace – Bonhoeffer was a Lutheran, after all –

but simply that a day without morning prayer runs the risk of descending into meaninglessness and randomness. This I may say is most definitely my experience. The days I wake to pray, 'awakening the dawn' as the Psalmist puts it, take on a particular shape and hue. The days I don't pray in the morning struggle to form in quite the same way. They end up random, thankless days, if not downright manic. It is as simple as that. The primeval mess of the opening sentences of Genesis reasserts its power and we are back into chaos. Instead of living attentively, gratefully, contentedly, we live anxiously and fretfully. This of course is the paradox of morning prayer: faced with a busy day, appointments to fulfil, e-mails to write, journeys to make, chores to finish, we avoid prayer, thus leaving ourselves open to the tyranny of the urgent. And even though a day without morning prayer may indeed be lived well, too many of them put together means that time seems to run away, anxieties accumulate, fears break in, and soon enough we are living in the middle of next week.

Beginning in prayer, however, opens up the possibility of a state of prayer – perhaps what Paul means by 'prayer without ceasing' – in which we are present for each and every situation, good or ill. For this is the day that the Lord has made, there is no other. This is the point of early morning prayer – the busier I am, the more I need to pray. When I do pray, strangely enough the busyness subsides, fears are stilled, and God is present to me. Only when we have closed down the horizons of the future and seek to pay attention to this day do we have any chance of living it well. Speaking about how he sustained a long and fruitful ministry as an activist bishop during the apartheid years in South Africa, Desmond Tutu mused: 'If your day starts off wrong, it stays skewed. What I've found is that getting up a little earlier and trying to have an hour of quiet in the presence of God, mulling over some scripture, supports me.'[23] Indeed, it is the special preserve of praying at the dawn of the day, in the hour between sleeping and waking, to announce not only the heralding of a new day, but, if our imagery is correct, 'the day-break colours of the future', as Jürgen Moltmann puts it.[24] I shall say more about this in chapter 9.

In thinking about prayer, it is important for me to say at this point something that was mentioned in the introduction: namely, that what we are talking about is not a schedule of prayer but

rather a rhythm of prayer. It would be rather easy to conclude
from what I have said that all I need to do is to schedule a time of
prayer, fit God into my busy day. But that is not what prayer is.
That is the reason why so many of our new year's prayer resolu-
tions fall to the ground. They are conceived on the enemy's terri-
tory of time management, and time itself is a form of tyranny. If
we are to have any chance of finding time to pray, then paradoxically we have to abandon the tyranny of *chronos* time, entering
instead into the liturgy of the hours.[25] Here, prayer is not so much
filling up an allotted time, but embracing the movements of God's
grace as they occur to us throughout the day. For our goal is not
simply an early morning prayer time – the proverbial evangelical
quiet time – but a day of prayer. Prayerfulness doesn't stop with
the end of our early morning prayer. It is only just beginning.

And There was Evening and There was Morning

One of the ways into this perhaps is to recognise that biblically
speaking the day doesn't begin with the morning anyway, but the
evening. God created the world, 'And there was evening and
there was morning, the first day . . . And there was evening and
morning, the second day . . . And there was evening and morning, the third day' – and so on, until the sixth day. In which case,
as Peterson reminds us, the morning is less something to be
grasped than it is something to be entered into.[26] We do not initi-
ate the day, for in one sense the day has begun without us. The
first thing we do in a day is sleep, watching the world enter into
darkness, returning to the dust from which we are made. We
wake to a world that has been going on in our absence, initiated
by another. And thus it is that all true Christian spirituality
thrives: in recognition that we enter into the grace begun by
another. The rhythm of evening and morning is itself a reflection
of the fact that grace is always prior to anything we contribute.[27]

According to this way of looking at the world, Christmas Eve
is probably the only day in our year that takes on this biblical
shape, for it is indeed the evening of Christmas. Maybe that is
why we love it so much. Quite apart from the fact that the magic
of Christmas Eve may have something to do with presents – a not

insubstantial factor when it comes to children of course – my suspicion is that the enchantment of Christmas Eve may also have something to do with the pleasing integrity of an evening being joined so forcibly and intentionally to the following morning.

Psalm 4 and Psalm 5 express this diastole and systole of Christian spirituality, reflected in Samuel Wesley's anthem *Lead me Lord* which is a conflation of the two psalms:

> Lead me Lord, lead me in thy righteousness,
> Make thy way plain before my face.
> For it is thou, Lord, thou, Lord, only
> That makest me dwell in safety.[28]

Psalm 4 ends with the Psalmist lying down to rest 'for you alone make me dwell in safety'; Psalm 5 begins with an expectation of the Lord's reply. In setting Psalm 4 alongside Psalm 5, the editor of the Psalms echoes the primordial shape of the creation story, where morning happens not in a vacuum, without context, but as an anticipation of grace. As Peterson says, 'We go to sleep, and God begins his work. As we sleep he develops his covenant. We wake and are called out to participate in God's creative action. We respond in faith, in work. But always grace is previous. Grace is primary. We wake into a world we didn't make, into a salvation we didn't earn.'[29] In Marilynne Robinson's elegiac novel *Gilead*, the old pastor of the church enacts this anticipation of grace through his practice of walking through the streets in the dark, letting himself into the church, and watching the dawn come into the sanctuary. As one who didn't sleep much, sometimes he would walk at one or two in the morning past the houses of the parish, remembering the people who lived in each one and praying for them. 'And I'd imagine peace they didn't expect and couldn't account for descending on their illness or their quarrelling or their dreams. Then I'd go into the church and pray some more and wait for daylight.'

Prayerful wandering in this way is, I guess, what a lot of Christians do.[30] There is a veritable tradition within the New Testament itself of prayer that is both day and night.[31] As the wise old pastor says, 'I've often been sorry to see a night end, even while I have loved to see the dawn come.'[32] Somewhere in the intersection of night passing into day, grace is enacted. In the night, Yahweh cuts covenant with Abraham, calling forth the family of faith;[33] in the night, God sets his people free from Pharaoh's tyranny;[34] in the night, Dagon's statue falls to the ground in the presence of the ark of God;[35] in the night, the gospel is announced to Joseph: 'the virgin shall be with child, and he will be called Immanuel'. And when he awoke, Matthew records, instead of divorcing her, he took her home until the baby was born.[36] As the Psalmist says: 'Let the morning bring me word of your unfailing love.'[37]

Who Am I?

The problem with this liturgical take upon our lives is that the first news we embrace in the morning is not the news of unfailing love, but the news emanating from the media. Often the first thing we do when we wake is fill our ears with the noise of the media, or scan the papers to see what is happening in the real world. Reflecting on this obsession for news Thomas Merton notes:

> The ritual morning trance, in which one scans columns of newsprint, creates a particular form of generalized pseudo-attention to pseudo reality. This experience is taken seriously. It is one's daily immersion in 'reality.' One's orientation to the rest of the world. One's way of reassuring himself that he has not fallen behind. That he is still there. That he still counts!

I think he is right. My first instinct on waking is to make a cup of tea, switch on the radio and listen to the news. But if early morning prayer is to have a chance of resurfacing in the Christian community some courage needs to be exercised here: courage to withdraw temporarily from this pseudo-world of modern media, not to mention the obsessive world of e-mail and the Internet, in order to attend to first things. Courage is the right word because withdrawal feels irresponsible. It feels as if one is out of touch. How can I belong, keep up, if I don't know what is going on in the real world? But as Merton so forcibly puts it: 'My own experience has been that renunciation of this self-hypnosis, of this participation in the unquiet universal trance, is no sacrifice to reality at all. To "fall behind" in this sense is to get out of the big cloud of dust that everybody is kicking up, to breathe and to see a little more clearly.'[38] Try it! Lo and behold, the world doesn't stop when we stop. It goes on just as before. My non-participation in the world of news media makes no difference to it at all. In fact, what non-participation does is create space to attend to true realities: God in Jesus Christ ruling and saving. The day begins not with the chatter of the breakfast news, nor the probing questions of the radio interviewer, but with the transcendent Lord himself who makes his announcement to the world: 'You are my Son, today I have become your Father.'[39]

Of course, this takes some believing. Since so much of our identity throughout the day is shaped by anything other than this primal, baptismal identity, it takes some time for these words to penetrate. As T.S. Eliot so memorably put it:

> Where shall the word be found, where will the word
> Resound? Not here, there is not enough silence.[40]

Picking up the early morning radio image once more, it is a bit like tuning in on the old analogue radios: it takes some time to get a good reception. When we pray 'Our Father' it is like twiddling the tuning button until finally, after five minutes, the crackle has gone and we can hear clearly.[41] Which all goes to say that probably the first thing we should do in prayer is to linger a while, until at last we believe. For prayer in the first instance, it is universally agreed, is not petition, nor confession, but contemplation of the glorious truth of my adoption. Maybe those American evangelists are on to something after all. When you stand before the mirror in the morning and look at that tired old face, tell yourself: at my core I am not a statistic, not a consumer, not simply a number on a payroll. I am a child of God.

5

Practising the Present

Teach me, my God and King,
In all things thee to see,
And what I do in any thing,
To do it as for thee.[1]

A man goes to the factory canteen Monday lunchtime, opens his lunchbox, and says to his mate who is sitting opposite: 'Cheese sandwiches.'

The next day, the same thing; he knocks off for lunch, opens his box, shrugs his shoulders, and moans to his mate: 'Cheese sandwiches.'

Wednesday and Thursday the same thing happens. Friday arrives, he sits down for lunch, takes out his sandwiches, and cries out 'Not again! Cheese sandwiches.'

At which point his mate finally remarks: 'Why don't you tell your wife to make something different?'

'Oh, she didn't make these,' he said. 'I did.'

Like all good sermon illustrations, this little cameo works on a number of levels. First, it is quite funny. Second, it makes its point quite well. In the Christian life we have responsibilities. We are not powerless to act. But it is the underlying fabric of the story that interests us most of all: the routine world of getting up and going to work, day after day after day, in which nothing seems to change. It is a world we all have to deal with one way or another, whether we are paid or unpaid, blue collar or white collar, nine to five or seven to eleven. The vast bulk of our lives will be preoccupied with work. And since most of us do not sit idly by, it is imperative that our marking of the hours includes it.

Given the ease with which Christian spirituality so often defaults to a semi-gnostic mood, it would be easy to conclude that this work thing – the commute up to London, the sitting down in front of a computer screen, the teaching in front of a class of eight-year-olds, the cleaning out of the bedpans, the clearing up the house and the preparation of meals – represents a journey away from the purity of the sanctuary to the profanity of the shop floor. Indeed whole swathes of Christian spiritual writing, and certainly preaching, are based on this false dichotomy. For the Christian, however, this ordinary time is no less spiritual than prayer, for work takes its cue from the God-ordained movements of the world. Just as the sun rises, and the nocturnal animals return to their dens, so 'man goes out to his work,' says the Psalmist, 'to his labour until evening'.[2] It lies within the providence of God. And even though most of us live some distance now from the Psalmist's world of 'springtime and harvest,'[3] so beautifully depicted by Ronald Blythe in the Wormingford diaries,[4] it is still possible, with a little imagination, to embrace a day of work, even in the city, with the same rural instincts. One doesn't have to be a farmer to appreciate the cycle of the seasons and the rhythm of a day. There is still just enough natural light left in our neon world to know the difference between morning and evening. What one does need is the ability to pay attention, to reverence the day, and 'Whatever you do, work at it with all your heart, as you are working for the Lord, not for men'.[5]

In this chapter I should like to affirm this dimension of our spiritual existence, making connections between work and worship, labour and prayer. Finding purpose and satisfaction in our labour is a huge part of what it means to live a day well. Even the master of the absurd, Qohelet, can see that: 'A man can do nothing better than to eat and drink and find satisfaction in his work.'[6] And whilst so much of our life can feel absurd, it will not be rescued by some flight of spiritual fancy. A God who vacates the world of the everyday is indeed no God at all, but merely the projection of our idle dreams.

On Having a Proper Job

Of course, some would argue that people like me are not best placed to write about work, not to mention preach about it. After all, it has been a while now since I had a proper job. A few years ago, between pastorates, I did what is commonly referred to as tent-making: working Monday to Friday for a friend of mine as a gardener.[7] Prior to that, however, my last proper job was back in 1990, when I worked as a secondary school teacher. It occurs to me that I haven't had a proper job for seventeen years. And even now, as a pastor, I only work one day a week, as everyone loves to tease me. So what do people like me know about work? It is a good question. One of the things that tent-making showed me was how easy it is for church leaders to become detached from the world of work.

How I overcome this is to ask myself the question before I step up into the pulpit each Sunday to deliver the sermon: 'What will these people be doing at 11 o'clock Monday morning? I know what I will be doing: usually enjoying a cup of coffee with Susanna having walked for an hour or so on the Surrey hills. Joking aside, we pastors do work hard, but Monday is my Sabbath, and lest the day ends up as a series of chores, the first thing we try to do every Monday morning is enjoy the fresh air. But for most of my congregation 11 o'clock Monday morning is work time, and rather than enjoying a quiet ramble on Pewley Down or Newlands Corner, 11 o'clock Monday will find them behind a computer screen, round the directors' table, driving a taxi, in the classroom, working the soil, or shopping at Tesco with the toddlers. This is what an ordinary weekday will involve. Hence the question: What are you doing at 11 o'clock Monday?

The question is not original to me, I have to say. I think I am right in saying that it was framed by a group of theologians at my old Bible College, the London School of Theology, as part of a drive to get students to think through the implications of their faith for the world of work. After all, this is the world that will preoccupy the lives of the people most of the would-be ministers would end up serving in church. People don't come to church on a Sunday pondering the exegetical nuances of Romans 6; more likely they will be pondering the statistical complexities of next day's spreadsheet. (Furthermore, the fact that the pastor has a head start in prayer is precisely how it should be. Why else are pastors on a stipend?) Thus, quite apart from the fact that so much of the Bible is set in the context of the everyday, to do theology in the pulpit in isolation from these concerns is to be guilty of the very worst kind of ecclesiastical introspection. As Mark Greene and others have been at pains to point out, we need a theology that thanks God for Monday.[8] As well as the one-day world of the preacher, we need a Monday celebration of the worker. A day bracketed by morning and evening prayer is all well and good. What we also need is a theology for the something in between.

The Abolition of the Laity

The place to start, therefore, in any spirituality of the ordinary is to admit the hierarchy that exists in many churches concerning what is spiritual and what is unspiritual: that is, work that is regarded as of spiritual importance and work that is simply work. In this respect, people like me do really well. As a pastoral leader of a Christian community I rank pretty near the top, as does my wife who used to be a nurse. Nursing, as with teaching, scores pretty highly in Christian communities, for there is a discernible link between the nature of the work and the moral vision of the Bible. Not so with business people, however; nor lawyers, nor engineers – nor for that matter housewives. They are consigned to the bottom of the pile, and as a result often feel totally detached from the worshipping life of the church.

Clearly we need a revision of what we are doing here. Whether this requires us to abolish all notions of clergy–laity, as some would advocate, I am not sure. Personally, I think those who talk about the abolition of the laity – such as Paul Stevens – are guilty of throwing the baby out with the bathwater.[9] Ecclesial ministry is a specific calling, and has both biblical and historic precedent. Such is the anti-clericalism that exists in the church that it is in more need of affirmation these days than at any other time in recent history. But where Stevens is right is that so often the affirmation of the calling to minister in the church has been at the expense of the sanctity of all other kinds of work – as if there was such as thing as spiritual work and secular work. The Bible knows nothing of such distinctions. There is simply work that is done unto the Lord, and work that isn't: which means that even the most menial work, as Luther and Calvin celebrated, can receive divine status, and even the most exalted ecclesiastical office can be nothing more than vanity. It all depends on who it is done for.[10]

What this means for a spirituality of the day is quite dramatic; for it suggests that even the most ordinary work day has huge possibilities for the life of faith. Work is not a means to a financial end; nor is it a means to some evangelistic end (as if the only way we can sanctify work is to see it as a launch pad for witnessing to colleagues). Although both of these ends have some validity, they end up trivialising work. Work is in and of itself part of our creaturely existence. To co-create with God is what we were made for and, furthermore, what we will be doing for eternity. When you go to work on a Monday morning, you are not entering deconsecrated ground; rather – if the liturgy of Sunday has anything to do with it, and if my early morning devotions have anything to do with it – you are sanctifying even the most mundane routine with Holy Spirit grace.

When David was anointed by Samuel the prophet to become Israel's king it is significant to learn that the next thing he does is return to the fields to shepherd the flock; a return to the days of obscurity from which he had come.[11] As far as David was concerned the anointing does not override the mundane but sanctifies it. The anointing does not cancel out the ordinary but transfigures it – even shepherd work. In fact, it would be many days of obscurity in the wilderness before David would take the throne from Saul; and the temptation is always to hurry it along. On more than one occasion David was presented with just such an opportunity.[12] But rather than seizing his future, as so many of us try to do, he learnt the secret of being content. Though he could have despised the endless days on the hillside, leading the sheep back and forth, or the days when he was on the run in the rocks and crags of En Gedi, he saw them as God ordained.

From our perspective we know the end. We know that David became king, establishing Jerusalem as his centre of worship, leading Israel into what many regard as its golden era. But David didn't know that. Most times all he knew was the back of a cave, or the back end of a sheep. And yet the Psalms record for us a man who had an acute sense of the holy; a man who learnt to sanctify the present:

My heart is not proud, O Lord, my eyes are not haughty; I do not concern myself with great matters or things too wonderful for me. But I have stilled and quietened my soul; like a weaned child with its mother, like a weaned child is my soul within me.[13]

The line between killing lions on the hillside and killing God's enemies in the valley was seamless, as far as David was concerned. He took as much pleasure in the lion's carcass as in Goliath's head.[14]

IFs and WHENs

Laying hold of David's contentedness might go a long way, perhaps, to eliminating the kind of conversations pastors have from time to time with people who see Christian ministry as a way out of the boredom of their own job. It doesn't happen that often, but once in a while you meet people who have this strange notion that compared to what they are presently doing Christian ministry is glamorous work, where the real action is, and what they should be doing for the rest of their lives. But that is just about the worst reason for entering the ministry. As I often say to people who idealise church work, being a pastor is not glamorous work: essential, to be sure, but not glamorous. The same could be said of missionary work. If a person cannot find contentedness in the work they are presently doing, there is slim chance they will find it in ministry. They would last about two weeks at most.

Eileen Crossman writes of the struggles James O Fraser, missionary to the Lisu tribe in the early part of the twentieth century, had in this regard. Ever tempted to relegate his training in engineering at Imperial College, London, as secondary to his missionary training, and then tempted to relegate his missionary training as inconsequential compared to the actual missionary work he wanted to do in China, Crossman notes that in his journal O Fraser reflects on the need to learn, like the apostle Paul, the secret of being content in every situation. 'It has come home to me very forcibly of late,' he writes, 'that it matters little what the work is in which we are engaged: so long as God has put it into our hands, the faithful doing of it is of no greater importance in

one case than in another . . . The temptation I have often to contend with is persistent under many forms: "If only I were in such
and such a position" for example, "shouldn't I be able to do a
great work! Yes, I am only studying engineering at present, but
when I am in training for missionary work things will be different and more helpful." '[15]

As far as O Fraser is concerned such a way of living is madden-
ingly elusive, 'it is all IF and WHEN,' whereas God calls us to
embrace whatever he places before us in life. 'I believe it is no more
necessary to be faithful (one says it reverently) in preaching the
Gospel than in washing up the dishes in the scullery. I am no more
doing the Lord's work in giving the Word of God to the Chinese than
you are, for example, in wrapping up a parcel to send to the tailor.'[16]

In our church we have a way of affirming this. Once in a while
someone in the congregation will be asked to speak for five minutes on a Sunday morning about the work that they do during
the week. So far, we have had an airline pilot, a head teacher, a
business director, a staff nurse, and an engineer. We ask our missionaries, as I somewhat provocatively refer to them, three questions: 'What is it that you do?' 'What are the challenges you face
as a Christian in your job?' and 'How can we as a church support
you?' Then we pray.

The last interview, with the engineer, is a case in point, because
he was about to go off on two weeks' unpaid leave with a missionary agency to visit prisons in the Philippines. This in itself was
worthy of a slot on a Sunday morning, particularly because he
wanted to raise money for the trip. Churches do this all the time,
and do it well. But what caught my interest was not so much the
trip to the Philippines, but his utter enthusiasm for the work he
did with the rest of his time as an engineer. This was his real passion, it turned out, and as far as I was concerned of equal importance to his trip to the prison, because of course being an engineer
is his daily experience. It is here, among men who think nothing
of compromising their morals to gain a quick buck, that his daily
cross-bearing becomes reality. Just as we might want to say that
marriage is not a distraction from discipleship but, for those who
are married, its very heart, so his work is not an adjunct to his discipleship – a tag on to his Christian activity, or even his missionary endeavours – it is the very essence of discipleship. Indeed,

what could be more missionary than working day after day in such an environment? As Greene asks, why do we always pray on a Sunday for someone going off to Saudi Arabia as a missionary, when tomorrow one of our congregation is going to a Kodak office in Harrow? 'The irony is that Kodak may be an unreached people-group every bit as needy as the Saudis.'[17]

These interviews on a Sunday, therefore, have become critical in shaping a truly Christian response to the world we are about to re-enter. They are both an affirmation of the weekday world we have come from, an anticipation of the world we are about to engage with. Furthermore, these interviews are a great way of relativising the pulpit, but in such a way that avoids disrespecting it. They claim a both/and rather than an either/or approach. The simple act of bearing witness to the world of work within the service brings the messiness of the factory floor into the sanctuary even as it sanctifies the same through the word of God and prayer. As Abraham Kuyper famously said in his inaugural address at the dedication of the Free University of Amsterdam: 'There is not a square inch in the whole domain of human existence over which Christ who is sovereign over all does not cry "Mine!"'[18] If I can't find the Lord in the workplace, what point is there seeking him in the garden. He will not be Jesus of Nazareth, but some figment of our pious imagination.

The Noonday Demon

Since the daily office has shaped a good deal of the reflections throughout the book, the morning and evening office in particular, it is worth noting that the noonday office of Sext is of particular relevance to what we are talking about here, related to what the desert fathers call the *daemon meridianus,* or 'demon of the noontide'. The noonday demon, according to Evagrius Ponticus, 'makes it seem that the sun barely moves, if at all, and that the day is fifty hours long,' and 'instils in the heart of the monk a hatred for the place, a hatred for his very life itself, a hatred for manual labour'.[19]

Anyone who has a regular, routine job will have known this feeling. In the anatomy of sin it is what the physicians of the soul

call *acedia*: boredom, frustration, lack of energy, whereupon any-
where else or anything else seems preferable to this work that I
am doing now. In the noonday office we pray against this boredom.[20] In the prayers of midday, in the middle of the working
day, we pray against our distractedness, our desire to escape, to
wish the time away. Along with my Benedictine friend, we pray
for stability, for contrary to what we might think the grass is not
greener somewhere else, anymore than the people are more
saintly somewhere else. There may be fresh opportunities, and
one day I may end up doing something other than what I am
doing now. But the noonday office calls me to fidelity to the work
I am doing now.

Again O Fraser:

> It is all IF and WHEN. I believe the devil is fond of those conjunc-
> tions . . . I have to-day, to a limited extent, the opportunities to
> which he has been putting me off (not that I have always yielded
> to these temptations), but far from helping me be faithful in the
> use of them, he now turns quite a different face. The plain truth is
> that the Scriptures never teach us to wait for opportunities of serv-
> ice but just to serve in the things that lie next to our hands.[21]

Work is not only an exercise of the body, but an exploration of the
soul: through daily service to whatever it is that lies next to our
hands, we learn fidelity, just as through attentiveness to whoever
sits next to me in church, we learn to love.

The Anglican priest George Herbert explores this idea in his
poem *The Elixir*, which sits at the beginning of this chapter. Using
the image of the mythical stone, Herbert reckons on a world in
which no matter how mundane or ordinary our work might be,
the simple act of offering it up to God 'turneth all to gold'. I
accept that this might be easier in certain jobs than others. The
connections between work and worship are more obvious in certain settings than others. Indeed, I met someone recently whose
description of what they did left me feeling utterly depressed by
the sheer monotony of it. Nevertheless, if Herbert is in any way
correct, there is a sense in which even the most mind-numbingly
boring job can become service, simply by the way we attend to it.
Indeed,

A servant with this clause
Makes drudgerie divine:
Who sweeps the room, as for thy laws,
Makes that and th'action fine.[22]

I can recall one or two jobs myself of the clock-watching kind. Every five minutes of the clock seemed like an eternity. But what Herbert is saying is that this need not be the case. Though the job might be menial, 'th'action' can become fine. Every five minutes can indeed be an eternity, not in the monotonous sense, but in a fulfilled sense. As Charles Wenmouth puts it in Peter Hobbs' debut novel, *The Short Dying Day*, 'There is a rhythm of work that carries me through the day the heavy ringing note constant as a heartbeat patterning my actions and consuming my thoughts so that the day passes rapidly.'

Wenmouth is a blacksmith and Methodist lay-preacher to boot, in the far reaches of south-west England near the end of the nine-teenth century. Wenmouth narrates his observations of the world around him and his own burning faith in God; in its own way the novel is a meditation on faith, time and eternity. But it is what he says about his work that is telling: 'It feels good. My attention taken up with it. Nothing else keeps in my mind but it is a noble state to be in it seems to balance my soul and set things right it is very rewarding.'[23] Approached correctly, work is a sanctifying rhythm.

Pouring Out the Oil of Love

Since this section of the book claims to track the liturgy of the hours it would seem logical at this point to speak about an act-ual prayer time during the day. And I do know of people who do precisely that: they steal into a quiet chapel at lunchtime, or go for a walk along a canal for ten minutes, in order to pray. But as laudable as this is, such practices are not the burden of this chap-ter. Attentiveness to God does not mean we have to be on our knees in prayer all the time. This has been the bane of evangeli-cal spirituality from the outset: as if the only way to be spiritual is to retire to a prayer closet for hours on end.

For sure, prayer must be intentional. I have never been fully convinced by those who say their prayer time is in the car on the way to work, or on the train. Jesus said 'But when you pray, go into your room, close the door and pray to your Father, who is unseen.'[24] Even so, prayer does not finish the moment we get up off our knees, so to speak. A life of prayer is only just beginning. We may not have the luxury of time during the day to set aside for prayer; but our day can still be prayerful – simply by the way we go about our tasks. Practising the presence of God, as Brother Lawrence reminds us,[25] can take place in front of the kitchen sink just as much as before the altar of God. Indeed a kitchen sink can become an altar. As Ruth Graham had over her kitchen sink, apparently: 'Divine service takes place here three times a day.' Work is not a distraction from the spiritual life; any more than marriage is. It *is* the Christian life. A proper liturgy of the hours is not just about finding God in prayer, but finding God in everything we do. 'I have no other will but God's will, which I seek to fulfil in all things,' says Brother Lawrence, 'and to which I am so committed that I would not wish to pick up a piece of straw without his command, and for any other motives than pure love of him.' Indeed, he goes on to say that 'I have abandoned all my forms of worship, and those prayers which are not obligatory, and I do nothing else but abide in his holy presence, and I do this by simple attentiveness and an habitual, loving turning of my eyes upon him.'[26] Although this, as an attitude of piety, skirts dangerously close to super-spirituality, nevertheless it insists that all of life, however trivial, comes under the purview of God. And unless we broaden our definition to include this, it is likely that many people in our churches will continue to feel disenfranchised from the life of faith.

For instance, a mother – or father for that matter – at home with little toddlers is unlikely to find huge amounts of time for prayer. Physical tiredness alone may well mean that prayer is in snatches, like Susanna Wesley who used to lift her apron over her head once in a while to signal to the children she was not to be disturbed. But does this mean a mother is disqualified from the spiritual life, condemned to a life of perpetual failure? Given the way that prayer is described in many of the classical presentations of the spiritual life, a modern day mother may well conclude that she is. Add to that a well-meaning exhortation from the pulpit about the noble wife of Proverbs 31 – 'she gets up while it is still dark'[27] – she may well conclude she is not even a Christian.

But if we define spirituality in terms of attentiveness to God, then there is no reason why anyone should feel excluded from the Christian life. In so far as loving one another is the ultimate expression of abiding in Jesus, then a well-timed act of kindness may mean as much to the Lord as a well-spoken prayer. Forsaking one's own needs for the sake of a little one, which is often what happens in family life, may mean as much to the Lord as the most glorious act of martyrdom. Again, it all depends on how we approach a thing. Chaos, as science is increasingly becoming aware, is not necessarily a bad thing.

For instance, I remember a mother in my last church bemoaning the state of her spiritual life. Alongside all the other 'spiritual' women in the church, she regarded herself as very feeble indeed. She didn't pray very much, didn't sing very well, and, what is more, couldn't speak in tongues. But on discovering that she had undertaken to care not only for her own children, but also for the child of another mother who was in hospital – arranging pick-ups for the other mother's child, providing regular meals when her friend returned home, and making sure her house was cleaned weekly – it struck me that her definition of 'spiritual' was skewed, to say the least.

Yes, there is a danger that the call to self-sacrifice can be overdone, to the point that it becomes destructive. But that aside, my point is that her doing was as formative as her praying. Even though I have spent some time emphasising that it is not what we do but who we are that defines our identity – and I firmly believe that to be the starting point of Christian formation – it must also be true that what we do is also a pretty good expression of who we are. After all, as John writes in one of his letters: 'If anyone has material possessions and sees his brother in need, but has no pity on him, how can the love of God be in him?'[28] More specifically, the parable of the Good Samaritan teaches us that oil and wine poured on a broken body in the heat of the day is as much worship as the oil and wine offered by the priest in the morning and evening sacrifices,[29] and oftentimes more telling. So whilst my anxious mother may not have had the luxury of a daily quiet time, there's no knowing how precious her daily routines are to the Lord.

In all of this I am not unmindful of the debate raging at the moment within the Christian community about mothers who return to work. Talking to mothers in the church, particularly those who have given up careers temporarily for the sake of children, I understand that one of the big challenges for some – though not all – is the often vacuous nature of baby care. And it may well be that some mothers need to return to work for their own sanity, not to mention the more serious question of vocation. Though it is something my wife and I have strong views about, the question of whether it is right for a mother with young children to go back to work is not something I have ever wanted to legislate upon in churches that I have led.

What I hope is obvious, however, from what I have written, is that neither option – staying at home or going to work – can avoid the challenge that we all face not to fantasise about being somewhere else, doing something else. In order to slay that dragon, what we require is not so much a change of situation but a change of heart. As Alie Stibbe discovered – struggling as a young mother of four children, and resentful of the limitations this imposed upon her – once we say 'yes' to our situation, even the kitchen can become holy ground.[30]

6

Abide With Me, Fast Falls the Eventide

Before the ending of the day,
Creator of the world, we pray
That you, with steadfast love, would keep
Your watch around us while we sleep.[1]

I guess most of us have been iconoclasts at one time or another: the desire to smash the establishment is strong among us nonconformists. In fact, in my student years at Durham, when my house church radicalism was at its highest, even the magnificent cathedral seemed nothing more than an empty shell to me. Anything that was vaguely ecclesiastical was met with contempt by us charismatic hotheads, and in a bishopric like Durham things ecclesiastical amounted to a good deal.

For those of us who were into this evangelical vigilante work, at the top of our hit list was night-time service of Compline, practised by the chapel boys. What kind of a service is that? It sounded more like a bedtime drink than a serious prayer time. There they would go, scurrying down to the ancient Norman chapel – located in the belly of Durham Castle – to recite their prayers whilst the rest of us would chatter on in the Undercroft bar. Whilst their day was ending with the *Nunc Dimittis* (Now let your servant depart in peace), ours was ending with the nine o'clock news. The idea of keeping a night-time office, or indeed any office of prayer, was anathema to us.

Now that I am older, however, I yearn for it. Or at least I yearn for the kind of closure on the day that something like the night-time office can bring. The older I get the less well I sleep. The more people I encounter, the less grace I seem to have. The more responsibilities I accumulate, the less likelihood of an uninterrupted night's sleep. I need completion.[2] Like many sleepless sufferers, frequently I wake in the night with a thousand different thoughts racing around my mind. And much as I try to count sheep, or imagine walking by the sea, it seems that trying to get back to sleep makes things worse. The harder you try, the worse it becomes. Consequently, without the refreshment of sleep, one day spills into another. We don't know if it is Monday or Friday. Any notion of 'This is the day that the Lord has made, I will rejoice and be glad in it,' is lost in a blur of muzzy-headedness, bleary eyes and cups of strong coffee.

I am not suggesting for one moment that the reinstitution of the night-time office is a cure for insomnia. That is not really my purpose in this chapter. Nor do I want to prescribe what people do with their evenings (any more than I want to prescribe what time they get up in the morning). But I do want to say with Merton that the quality of our night is inextricably linked to the activity of the day. In December 1963 Merton wrote: 'it becomes very important to remember the quality of one's night depends on the thoughts of the day . . . I bring there the sins of the day into the light and darkness of truth to be adored without disguise.'[3] In short, the way we live the day and, more specifically, the way we reflect back on the day, has everything to do with the way we put the day to bed. Furthermore, the way we close a day has everything to do with the way we begin the next. If I have slept well, there is every likelihood that I will live well. In this chapter, therefore, which is our third chapter devoted specifically to a liturgical hour, I should like to explore what kind of things sleeping Christianly might involve. If we are to live a day well, it seems to me that we need to learn to sleep well; or conversely, if we are to sleep well, we must learn to live well. Night passes into day as day passes into night. They form the heartbeat of a distinctively Christian approach to life.

A Theology of Sleep

It is an oddity, is it not, that there is very little written about sleep? Even though we spend a good deal of our time asleep or preparing for sleep, there has hardly been any reflection within the Christian community on its theology. Presenting his text to the reader, John Baillie notes,

> I think we hear far too few sermons about sleep. After all, we spend a very large share of our lives sleeping. I suppose that on average I've slept for eight hours out of every twenty-four during the whole of my life, and that means I've slept for well over twenty years. Don't you agree then that the Christian gospel should have something to say about the sleeping third of our lives as well as the waking two-thirds of them?[4]

Yet, a scouring through the major theological works of the Christian tradition will yield very few returns.

Such a situation is symptomatic, in my opinion, of our general disregard of the day itself, and the rhythms we are enjoined to live by. Once we decide that life is ours to grasp rather than something to be grateful for, something to attack rather than a gift to receive, then it is little wonder that night-time becomes a problem. Night-time commits the ultimate heresy for moderns: getting us to stop. To sleep well one has to relinquish, to let go. And since letting go is not something we are good at, many of us don't sleep very well.

We know this is the case simply by the statistics on the number of people who suffer from insomnia; even in the average Christian congregation there are vast numbers of people who complain of not being able to sleep. At the risk of offending (because of course there are good medical reasons why some people do not sleep well), one of the issues is control. It is about who runs the world. Whether I sleep well – like Jesus in the midst of the storm – depends to a large degree on whether I trust the competency of the Father.[5] 'He gives his beloved sleep,' says the Psalmist,[6] but if I insist on eating the bread of anxious toil, there is little chance I will enjoy this promise. More likely I will be condemned to a life of 'get up early and stay up late', with the sleep in between nothing more than a pause.

Sleep, however, should not be experienced in such shrivelled terms. As the Psalmist says, it is a gift. It is as much to be embraced, as the dawn is to be announced. As I stated earlier, the lying down of the evening prayer in Psalm 4 – 'for you alone make me dwell in safety' – is the essential prelude to the 'you wake me in eager expectation' of the morning prayer in Psalm 5, and to miss the one is to negate the other. Morning prayer depends on evening rest; evening rest prepares for morning prayer. These are the basic rhythms of the prayer-filled life. But more particularly, the shadow of the evening light, leading into night-time darkness, is an invitation to relinquish what power we have, resting once more in the knowledge that it is only God who 'neither slumbers nor sleeps,'[7] and therefore only God who can effectively run the world. As Robert Farrar Capon says: 'There's no point objecting to the rhythms of life and death . . . we can only "join the dance, As it moves in perichoresis, Turns about the abiding tree." '[8] In other words, we need to fall in.

Farrar's quotation is from W.H. Auden's monumental poem *Horae Canonicae*, in which the poet frames the Good Friday event, 'the abiding tree,' within the liturgy of the hours: Prime, Terce, Sext, Nones, Vespers, Compline, and Lauds. It was arguably his most important work, and the poem he spent the longest time developing: seven years in all. In it Auden explores the power of the existential moment, in which the past and the future are gathered up into the eternal now of Christ's passion. *Horae Canonicae* tracks an ordinary day, to be sure, but a day that is ordered, nonetheless, by the rhythm of the monastery. As such, it enables Auden to note in the day some powerful Christian impulses. If the hour of Prime is when

> at the vaunt of dawn, the kind
> Gates of the body fly open
> To its world beyond,

so Compline is the hour when

> Now, as desire and the things desired
> Cease to require attention,
> As, seizing its chance, the body escapes,
> Section by section, to join
> Plants in their chaster peace which is more
> To its real taste, now a day is its past,
> Its last deed and feeling in, should come

The instant of recollection
When the whole thing makes sense.[9]

What Auden is saying – I think – is that a day is not without content or shape. It is not a vacuous hole waiting to be filled. Rather, a day is given to us. Its various moods, the changing of the light, the rhythm of work and rest, are ordained by the gracious hand of God. So instead of fighting it, the challenge is to fall into line with it, recognising with the Psalmist that not only is the day yours, but 'yours also is the night'.[10]

Along with the Psalmist, Auden sees the evening of our day, our embrace of the night, as practice for death. If we fear dying we ought to fear going to sleep; for putting one's head on the pillow at night is a kind of rehearsal for the day when our bodies really will be put to rest. It is an act of faith. Just as I believe that God will one day resurrect this stuff of my body, and usher it into the new day of the new creation, so in sleep I relinquish control to God, in confidence that in his good time he will wake me again into the new day of his grace. As Simon Chan puts it: 'As we enter deeply into the rhythm of morning and evening prayer, we are reminded that the Christian life is not governed by the vicissitudes of optimism or pessimism that characterize the way of this world. Rather, Christian life is lived in hope in the midst of death.'[11] The cry in Psalm 90 for God to 'satisfy us in the morning with your unfailing love' can only be fully understood against the backdrop of sleep, death, and the eternity of God.[12]

Thus, sleep becomes part of a rhythm in which I am called upon daily to rehearse the central themes of the Christian gospel: death and resurrection. Viewed through the lens of Christian understanding we finally realise that each morning is a gift. The fact that we wake up at all is astonishing – not literally of course, for as Auden reminds us, we will in all likelihood wake to another day. Auden concludes *Horae Canonicae*, not with the service of Compline but with Lauds (3 a.m.), the first office of a new day, reminding us of the all too repetitive and mundane nature of our lives. But by paying attention to the grace that is at work in this night-and-day rhythm, in this ever so ordinary life, the new morning heralds promise: 'Bright shines the new sun on creatures mortal.'

Indeed, I would have to say that without the psychological help of night-time relinquishment and morning renewal I doubt that I would have got very far as a Christian. Contrary to what many of my congregation think, I struggle with all the same things as they do, and oftentimes fail just as badly. But God in his ordinance of the world causes the sun to go down, the sun to rise, and then the sun to go down again. What keeps me going is the knowledge that however awful today has been, tomorrow is another day. The people who frequent Christian pulpits or the platforms of Christian conferences are not holier than thou. Far from it. It's simply that they have learnt to live to fight another day. As Annie Dillard puts it in *Holy the Firm*: 'Every day is a god, each day is a god, and holiness holds forth in time. I worship each god, I praise each day splintered down, splintered down and wrapped in time like a husk, a husk of many colours spreading, at dawn fast over the mountains split.'[13] Poetic licence aside, she is right. Each day comes fresh. His mercies are new every morning. The fact that our lives are a series of night-to-day, light-to-darkness exchanges means there is always tomorrow. And since there is always tomorrow, today can be itself.

Do Not Let the Sun Go Down on your Anger

I am conscious, naturally, that all of this is far too mystical – dangerously so perhaps. Waxing lyrical about the night-time is one thing; but what we really want to know is 'Yes, but how?' In fact YBH could be written in the margins of just about every page of the book. And to some extent I have sought to address that, without being overly prescriptive. However, unless we engage in a little theologising about sleep, all we will end up with is a few moral exhortations, but no real understanding of the importance of sleep in the Christian tradition. Without a little theologising about sleep we will do what we often do in the church: namely, offer up nothing more than a thinly disguised version of behavioural science. Whatever practical advice about sleep we give ought only to be understood within the wider framework of darkness and light, death and resurrection, relinquishment and renewal.

Furthermore, the images are not that difficult to grasp. The fact that evening opens us up to thoughts of mortality is not particularly original, any more than the connection between morning and thoughts of resurrection. We have already seen how images of sleep and death commingle in the Psalms, how images of light and darkness surface in the passion narratives, and also how these same themes appear within the Christian tradition that flows from them. Andrewes, whose *Private Devotions* we have looked at before in the context of morning prayer, and which Merton used to read in the night, made good use of the images, viewing these intersections of the day, quite legitimately, within the specifically Christian notion of death and resurrection. Hence, with reference to the evening of our lives, he writes:

> Having spent the day,
> I give Thee thanks, O Lord.
> Evening draws nigh;
> make it bright.
> As day has its evening,
> so also has life;
> the evening of life is age;
> age has overtaken me,
> make it bright.
> Cast me not off in the time of old age;
> forsake me not when my strength faileth.
> Even to my old age be Thou He,
> and even to hoar hairs carry me;
> do Thou make, do Thou bear,
> do Thou carry and deliver me.
> Abide with me, Lord,
> for it is toward evening,
> and the day is far spent
> of this toilful life.
> Let Thy strength be made perfect
> in my weakness.
>
> The day is fled and gone;
> life too is going,
> this lifeless life.
> Night cometh;
> and cometh death,
> the deathless death.[14]

Strangely, Andrewes places these evening prayers in a category of their own. They do not form part of the six days, but feature at the end as a kind of addendum. However, as far as he is concerned they are just as important as the morning prayers of the seven days of creation: 'And the mind of man, as it must be stirred up in the morning, so in the evening, as by a note of recall, is it to be called back to itself and to its Leader by a scrutiny and inquisition or examination of self, by prayers and thanksgiving.'[15]

Given the confessional nature of Anglican prayer, this is clearly Andrewes at his Anglican best. In a memorable phrase Andrewes warns us that 'The heart is deceitful above all things. The old man is bound up in a thousand folds. Therefore take heed to thyself'[16] – a sentence worthy of old Cranmer himself. In practical terms, it is the conjunction of evening prayer and confession – the kind of intro-spection that ought to hit us at the end of our life, replayed on a daily basis as we prepare to fall asleep. Andrewes reminds us, in true Anglican fashion, that the quality of our sleep is determined not only by our ability to let go, but also by the way we examine ourselves, for whatever else the speed of modern living has done it has left us car-rying around a backlog of unresolved angst. Our lives roll from one day to the next, accumulating debris like a tornado, until one day it all catches up with us in one almighty disaster. Had we stopped, however, at the end of each day, to release our fears and confess our sins, we may have avoided it. Not without good reason, Paul enjoins the Christians in Ephesus not to 'let the sun go down on your anger' (surely the best evidence yet that Paul at one time must have been married),[17] because the Lord created us to live one day at a time,[18] and to carry anger over through the night is to give the devil a foothold, that can eventually become a legion. As Plutarch puts it, 'We should next pattern ourselves after the Pythagoreans, who, though related not at all by birth, yet sharing a common discipline, if ever they were led by anger into recrimination, never let the sun go down before they joined right hands, embraced each other and were reconciled.'[19] Indeed a similar practice is enjoined on the Essenes in the Damascus Rule: 'They shall rebuke each man his brother according to the com-mandment and shall bear no rancour from one day to the next.'[20] Anger must not be allowed to smoulder overnight.

Although I can count on one hand the number of times I have actually participated in a service of Compline, it is immediately apparent that the last office of the day is particularly focused on this need to resolve the day's anguish in some form of forgiveness. Though a short service, it packs a powerful punch by forcing us to face up to the injuries perpetrated against us as well as the injuries we have inflicted on others. In the evening of our day we pray about them, asking for the grace to release ourselves and others from the anguish that even one ordinary day can hold. Appealing once again to monastic tradition, in the evening devotions Bonhoeffer notes the practice of the abbot begging the forgiveness of the brothers 'for all the faults and defaults committed against them'. Likewise, after their assurance to him of forgiveness, they beg the abbot for forgiveness of their faults and defaults, and receive forgiveness.

Quoting Ephesians 4:26 himself, Bonhoeffer warns: 'It is a decisive rule of every Christian fellowship that every dissension that the day has brought must be healed in the evening. It is perilous for the Christian to lie down to sleep with an unreconciled heart.'[21] How many churches have been shipwrecked by the simple refusal of certain members to engage in the basic ABC of Christian faith: reading the Bible, praying and forgiving? How many marriages have been destroyed on the simple grounds of unresolved anger? In the words of Thomas Browne 'Let not the Sun . . . go down upon thy wrath, but write thy wrongs in Ashes. Draw the curtain of night upon injuries, shut them up in the Tower of Oblivion, and let them be as though they had not been.'[22] Otherwise, tomorrow is ruined before it has even started.

On My Bed I Remember You

Practically speaking, not only is it important to clear our hearts of unresolved angst before we go to sleep, but it is also critical, if sleep is to be retrieved as a part of our Christian discipleship, to be more intentional about what we fill our minds with. Remembering God on my bed, and to 'think of you through the watches of the night',[23] is not some pious boast, but a godly intention to match one's public devotion with something equally sincere in the secret place of the night. What we think about in the night, when we rest our head on the pillow, is as good a yardstick as any of the nature of our worship, and also a prelude to the possibility of sleep as communion.

For instance, rather than watching late-night TV, try reading a Psalm once in a while or even just listening to the silence. It may well be that you sleep more deeply, and even dream more sweetly, since the last thought you take into your sleep is gospel-shaped rather than media-driven. After all, spiritual formation is not simply a day-time activity, but a night-time foray. As Baillie reminds us, with reference to the giants of the faith: 'These old worthies went to the centre at once. When they laid their heads upon their rude pillows, they remembered God. When they composed themselves to sleep, they were thinking upon his Word. And if they woke in the middle of the night it was to meditate upon his precepts.'[24]

This raises the question about what time we go to bed. My wife Susanna comes from a family where ten o'clock is holy hour – on the button. You can be in the middle of a conversation, but as soon as the clock turns ten, it's time for bed. Now, for someone who is out four nights out of seven – as many pastors are – this is a practical impossibility. Often I am not in until well after ten o'clock, and then there is the need to wind down. So, to aid this process, one year we broke with our habit and bought a television, primarily so I could watch something before going to bed. What I found, however, after an hour of watching sport and the late-night news, was that I was more tired in the morning than if I had simply read a page or two, brushed my teeth, got undressed and gone to bed.

So after twenty years of struggling with unfamiliar bedtime routines, I now look back with gratitude. I now realise you can't burn the candle at both ends. Had I insisted on late nights as well as early mornings, with my minimum seven hours' sleep reduced to six, I really would be eating the bread of anxious toil. In addition, had I continued with my practice of late-night viewing, I reckon I would have had a much harder time staring my congregation in the face. Holy living is hard at the best of times; add to that a late-night viewing schedule of boobs and bums, it is well nigh impossible. Eventually, I may have succumbed.

Once again, as with Sabbath observance, we are back with the issue of discipline. If grace precludes disciplines, then all I have written is completely irrelevant. More than that, it is harmful. But if grace includes it, then talking about what time we go to bed, what time we get up, and what we do last thing at night is hugely important. For instance, someone asked me the other day what I consider to be the most important aspect of Sunday worship. My answer: the time we go to bed the night before. If gathering on a Sunday really is special, then what I do with my Saturday evening is hugely important. I do not mean to act as a killjoy in saying so. For all I care Saturday night might mean a dinner party among friends; or a night out at the theatre; or a passionate embrace between couples. Why not? But in order for sleep to take its proper place within Christian formation, it seems to me that we will have to start protecting it from the ill-discipline of a 24/7 world.

He Gives his Beloved Rest

It occurs to me now, as we come to the end of this section, and this last of the liturgical hours, that in many ways sleep is a crucial aspect of Christian witness. How we sleep, or at least how we approach sleep, tells us everything about whether a person lives by grace or by works. Like the Sabbath, far from being a bolt on to our otherwise frenetic activity, sleep is the pivot upon which spiritual formation really thrives. The refrain in Genesis 1: 'And there was evening and there was morning,' is not just a quaint way of conceiving the day – namely, rest before work – but a radical reorientation towards God; for it is God who is at work in the night, not me. As we noted in our chapter on morning prayer, God's great covenantal acts oftentimes occur in the night. As Peterson puts it:

> While we sleep, great and marvelous things, far beyond our capacities to invent or engineer, are in process – the moon marking the seasons, the lion roaring for its prey, the earthworms aerating the earth, the stars turning in their courses, the proteins repairing our muscles, our dreaming brains restoring a deeper sanity beneath the gossip and scheming of our waking hours. Our work settles into the context of God's work. Human effort is honoured and respected not as a thing in itself but by its integration into the rhythms of grace and blessing.[25]

In short, what we do with the night is a clue to whether we live by our own agenda, or whether we live for the Kingdom of God. By going to sleep we let God do his greatest work in our lives, humbling us into recognition that the world I wake up to is not of my making.

If a 24/7 world has all but obliterated the rhythms of night and day, then a crucial aspect of Christian witness in this next generation is to restore them. We may not have to go as far as the monastics: in some instances their liturgical take on life led them to sleep in their coffins! But by taking sleep seriously as a dimension of Christian formation it may mean, when we wake at two in the morning, besieged by a thousand different thoughts, that rather than trying to marshal them into some semblance of order we should simply do the Christian thing and go dead.[26] We simply relinquish control. Like the preacher who paces around before the sermon, anxious over his delivery, the message, the congregation, we recognise that a better way to proceed is to simply go dead, to practice dying, in trust that when the day arrives God will be there.

I have a theory that most children's books are conspiracies by parents to get their children to sleep. Children's authors and parents, I believe, collude in the eternal battle of convincing a child that sleep is a good thing – pretty much all of them, if you haven't already noticed, end up with the main character tucked in bed and drifting off to sleep. Indeed, at one time or another all of my children had problems getting off to sleep when they were young, and there was nothing I loved more than telling them some bedtime story. But I would always ensure the lead character ended up asleep. Although they don't claim to be, children's bedtime stories are like Compline. Like all good family routines, such as 'please and thank you' around the dinner table, they are a kind of liturgy.

Speaking of his own difficulties in getting to sleep and the myriad of thoughts that attack us, Capon writes of his own bedtime reading: the practice of reciting the Suspice of St Ignatius of Loyola.

> Accept, O Lord my entire liberty,
> my memory, my understanding, and my will.
> All that I am and have, you have given me,

and I give back to you to be governed by your will.
Give me only the joy of your love and the comfort of your grace;
with these I am rich enough, and I ask nothing more.

In no way could the Suspice of Ignatius be construed as a bedtime story. That would be sentimentality in the extreme. But it
has the same effect, I believe, as a Father doting over his child in
bed. 'That prayer reminds me,' says Capon, 'that I didn't get into
bed with a right to eight hours' sleep, only with the privilege of
being who I am, as I am, for as long as I'm there. And I get that
notion from Jesus in the tomb.'[27]

INTERLUDE

Praying the Psalms

Blessed is the man
Who does not walk in the counsel of the wicked,
or stand in the way of sinners,
or sit in the seat of mockers.
But his delight is in the law of the Lord,
And on his law he meditates day and night.[1]

Having considered the rhythm of a day, it occurs to me that something needs to be said at this point – by way of an excursus – about the Psalms and their place in a rhythm of prayer. This book is peppered with psalms because for me the Psalms form the basis of my daily prayer, and have done so for many years: 'Evening, morning and noon I cry out in distress, and he hears my voice,' says the Psalmist.[2] And for me, as for many others, this crying out in distress has more often than not been through the primal language of the Psalms themselves. We have other ways of praying, of course: the Lord's prayer, praying in tongues, silent prayer, centring prayer, the Jesus prayer, Ignatian prayer. All of these are important and necessary.[3] I have written elsewhere about the importance of recovering the Lord's prayer for Christian discipleship. But when it comes to daily prayer, the book of Psalms is invariably where a day begins for me, in the classical Benedictine five psalms a day, making a hundred and fifty psalms a month cycle.[4]

The monthly journey through the Psalms is an interesting one. Having prayed them for nearly ten years now there is definitely more of an order to them than first meets the eye. It is not a systematic theology; that much is clear. But neither are the

Psalms completely random in their arrangement. Certain
themes cluster in particular places; certain words recur again
and again. The journey from Psalm 1 to Psalm 150 is *the* original
odyssey: from the safety of a world where the righteous flour-
ish and the wicked perish,[5] to a world where the wicked pros-
per and the righteous suffer,[6] all the way through to a world
where, whatever our experience of life, however unjust life has
been, all ends in praise.[7] To pray the Psalms over a month is to
embrace the whole gamut of human experience. As Calvin put
it in a preface to his commentary: the Psalms are 'an anatomy of
all parts of the soul'.[8]

Learning the Grammar of Faith

Coming from a tradition where extempore prayer was the norm,
praying the Psalms in a daily cycle of five psalms a day was
strange at first. It didn't seem like prayer. In fact, in the early days
of trying to pray the Psalms I would read a psalm out loud (a
practice which I would encourage, incidentally), and then, since
prayer and psalmody were, at that time, two quite different
things in my mind, I would pray about something else other than
the psalm. Having persisted off and on for ten years, however,
and having eventually realised that simply muttering the words
is actually a legitimate way of praying, the practice of praying the
psalm is now part of my body clock, as they say – part of the bio-
rhythm of my day. Waking up to whatever five psalms are before
me is like waking up to greet old friends. I have been here before.
I have heard these words already. Their familiarity is a comfort to
my soul, and a relief from having to find the right words.

Not that prayer should never be extempore. Crying out from
the heart is the very essence of prayer. In fact one of the spin-offs
of praying the Psalms is that at any point the one praying can
wander off with a word, or a sentence, and never actually finish
the psalm. But always the psalm is there to tutor us in what to say,
and how to say it. As Peterson says, with reference to the Psalms:
'Liturgy defends us against the commonest diseases of prayer: the
tyranny of our emotions, the isolationism of our pride.' I would
add to that: liturgy delivers us from the burden of intimacy which

is so much a part of my tradition. Though I am all for intimacy, to set out to be intimate in prayer is like the way we set out to have a great worship experience. It ruins it. Intimacy happens best when we give ourselves unselfconsciously to the steps by which it may happen or it may not. As Peterson continues: 'Liturgy pulls us out of the tiresome business of looking after ourselves and into the exhilarating enterprise of seeing and participating in what God is doing.'[9]

We might balk at his approach. Surely prayer is about what I am feeling. True. But many times we don't know what we feel and we don't know what to pray. We need words, even as other times we need to pray with groans that words cannot express (I am one of those who think that when Paul talks about praying 'with groans that words cannot express' he is referring to the gift of tongues). And what the Psalms provide us with are words to answer God with. That we don't identify with the particular mood of the psalm for that day, as is often the case, is not a problem according to this tradition of praying. Prayer is not in the first instance about my feelings anyway. I may identify with it, I may not. It doesn't matter. The point of liturgy, as Heschel reportedly said to his congregation on one occasion, was not to express what they felt; rather it was to learn what the liturgy expressed.

In a strange and paradoxical way, this liturgical rhythm of prayer, far from suppressing the emotions, in fact liberates them. As Kathleen Norris remarks, following her year-long exposure to the Psalms in a Benedictine monastery: 'To your surprise you find that the Psalms do not deny your feelings, but allow you to reflect on them, right in front of God and everyone.'[10] The reason for this is simple. As the British Benedictine Sebastian Moore reminds us, 'God behaves in the Psalms in ways that he is not allowed to behave in systematic theology.'[11] Our emotions are allowed to run wild. For those of us reared in the language of sentimental niceness on the one hand, and theological correctness on the other, the Psalms tutor us in a language that is far more daring. Without betraying the core of Israel's faith, the Psalms say it straight. They say our anger, just as they say our thanks. They say our sin, just as they say our wonder. They say our doubts, just as they say our faith. What the Psalms provide us with is a way to be human even as they provide a way to be holy. The one implies the other.

It is no surprise to me, therefore, that people instinctively turn to the Psalms when they are suffering. How many times have I been aware as a pastor of how critical the Psalms have become for someone going through treatment for a cancer, another facing a bereavement, another off work with stress, still another waiting for an unfaithful spouse to return? Each one of them testifies to the relevance of these ancient words; for what the Psalms do is transfer us from the flatness, dishonesty and inadequacy of so much of our modern speech and into the ancient and extreme world of praise and lament, with all the ambiguity that living at the extreme implies.

For instance, sometimes the depression never lifts, as in Psalm 88. Elsewhere, especially towards the end of the psalter, it seems as if the praise is overdone. For someone going through hard times, those Hallelujah Psalms sound like the shrill voice of a TV evangelist. But always the Psalms insist on raw words and images – nothing trite. Through the Psalms our laments are dragged from despair into hope; likewise, they usher us into our praises by declaring our grief. They provide us with a grammar of faith and a way of living one day at a time. For a generation that is desperate for roots, praying the Psalms puts one in touch with the deep bedrock of the earth. It centres our prayers in the prayers of the people of God.

When in 1978 Anatoly Sharansky was convicted on charges of treason and spying for the United States, ending up in a Siberian labour camp for nine years after sixteen months of incarceration, it is significant that he pleaded with the authorities not to strip him of his book of Psalms.[12] In truth, he was in the process of rediscovering his Jewish roots, hence the Psalms. But that is the point isn't it? Praying the Psalms puts us in the company of the ancient people of God, the Ancient of Days himself, who at his most critical hour gushed forth the words of a Psalm. It was in his blood. 'My God my God why have you forsaken me' was not Jesus proof-texting from the cross, but the heartfelt cry of a man steeped in the Psalms.[13] In fact, every time I get to that Psalm, on the fifth day of the month, I pause. It is like a station of the cross. To know that we are praying the same words of Jesus from the cross is to anchor our ordinary lives at the centre of all things: in the love of God.

All the Psalms, christological or otherwise, have this same effect. Before the world gets its teeth into us, the Psalms do their own work of slowing us down, getting us to see 'heaven in ordinarie'.[14] Instead of bringing God into our world, the Psalms invite us into their world: a world of salvation, grace, trust, thanksgiving, lament, and praise. As Sharansky himself said to his friend Mendelevich during a snatch of a conversation in the prison: 'I have a Passover Haggadah. I'm reading it. It helps me to learn the language. I already know the Psalms that are found there. It strengthens my soul because I learn from the faith and heroism of King David. What a wonderful man. And he is held in this stinking prison!'[15]

When I pray the Psalms the whole company of saints is there with me: those who have gone before and those who are here now. Furthermore, even if I don't feel what the Psalmist is going through, you can bet that someone else in the community of faith is. Even if I wake up joyful, for a change, and can't hack why the Psalmist is so downcast – 'why are so you downcast, O my soul?'[16] – the simple act of praying the Psalm reminds me that 'no man is an island.' It confronts me with the fact that I am part of a community in which at any one time there are people grieving even as I am rejoicing. Conversely, while I am grieving, there are others who are rejoicing. Praying the Psalms tutors us in this community awareness.

Sometimes when I am praying a psalm a face will appear; someone for whom this Psalm describes actual experience. Other times the words of the Psalm sound for all the world like the latest news bulletin from Kosovo, or the Congo, and so, in a strange way, the ancient liturgy helps me to be more up-to-date than I would otherwise be. Precisely because the world hasn't changed much, and human experience is awful a lot of the time, praying the Psalms, far from representing a retreat into private interiority, is an advance onto the concourse of life.

Bedside Prayers

It has been a common practice over the years to attach the book of Psalms to a pocket version of the New Testament. I guess the idea is that the Psalms are so universally popular and so commonly prayed that they are an essential companion to the gospel story. I have one of these versions myself and take it with me on most of my hospital visits. And there are no prizes for guessing which of the Psalms are most often read at the bedside. After years of doing this I can testify first-hand to the power of these ancient words. Reading Psalm 139 at the graveside of a person who died by suicide convinced me long ago that what the church needs in its public ministry, not to mention its public worship, is the gravitas of these ancient prayers: prayers where the words are weighty enough to hold us, cavernous enough for us to hide in.

In that sense they need no explanation. As C.S. Lewis noted in his *Reflections on the Psalms*: 'no historical readjustment is required. We are in the world we know.'[17] They simply need to be heard. 'Sing to one another in psalms, hymns and spiritual songs,' says the apostle Paul,[18] precisely because this is what the Psalms were meant for. They both tutor and guide us. Sung in the morning they set my bearings for the day to come; sung in the midst of a busy day, they slow us down; sung in the evening they bring the whole of the day into the light of God's presence.

Again, this is not the only way to pray. There are times when I haven't prayed the Psalms at all. But always the Psalms are there. Once prayed, the Psalms become part of our muttering life. We carry them round with us, in the pockets of our unconscious. So even when my mind has gone, and even when I cannot even remember my name, at the very deepest place of my identity the Psalms keep me rooted: in God, in place and in people.

In the film *The Elephant Man*,[19] set in the late nineteenth century, and cleverly filmed in black and white for effect, we see this power of psalmody to do this protective work wonderfully illustrated in the person of John Merrick, a circus freak taken into medical care by Treves, a doctor played by Anthony Hopkins. Though his colleagues are sceptical, Treves is convinced that this monstrous figure before him is indeed a human being, though goodness knows what trauma he has been through. He never says a word. He just stares blankly into space, thus confirming to all who examine him he is nothing more than an imbecile. If only Treves can get him to speak. Then, just as he is about to give up and consign his philanthropic project to the dust-heap, the Elephant Man speaks. What he utters in that first sentence explains why he has survived all those years. In the most polite English accent, and quoting from the King James, of course, he calls forth from deep within him the word that has kept him:

> The Lord is my shepherd; I shall not want.
> He maketh me to lie down in green pastures:
> he leadeth me beside the still waters.
> He restoreth my soul:
> he leadeth me in the paths of righteousness for his name's sake.
> Yea, though I walk through the valley of the shadow of death, I will fear no evil:
> for thou art with me; thy rod and thy staff they comfort me .
> Thou preparest a table before me in the presence of mine enemies; thou anointest my head with oil; my cup runneth over.
> Surely goodness and mercy shall follow me all the days of my life: and I will dwell in the house of the Lord for ever.[20]

PART THREE:

GLIMPSES OF THE DAY

7

Give us Today our Daily Bread

A part of me is dying. I am standing in the chilled-food aisle of a Tesco supermarket. I think I can feel my soul wither. But this is my neighbourhood. I should feel comfortable and at home.[1]

These days, it seems, only the French gather bread daily. Every morning, whether in the small villages of Picardy or in the large cities like Paris, French people make their routine trip to the local boulangerie to buy freshly baked baguettes. The *pain quotidien* is almost a 'sacramental cult'.[2]

Speaking as an Englishman, it is one of the great pleasures of holidays in France to enter into this daily ritual, trying out what French we know with the local shopkeeper. Having grown up in Tescoland (what my home town of Amersham is called by the locals by virtue of the supermarket that dominates the landscape), the trip to the local boulangerie is like one of those holiday romances: a brief but pleasant flirtation with a world that you know is not going to last, which probably doesn't exist – since France is no less consumerist than Britain – but which is enchanting nonetheless. Waking up in the morning in a small French village, leaving the house to walk to the boulangerie, and returning back with two or three baguettes under one's arm, definitely has something biblical about it – as does getting up early in the morning, as I do at home, to the delicious smell of bread baking in the kitchen.

It is that biblical instinct of trusting and thanking God for daily bread that I want to explore in this chapter – an ambitious proposal, to say the least. Who in Western consumerist societies would ever feel the need to pray this prayer? Our alienation from the land and from the rural cycle of sowing and harvesting renders it somewhat redundant. Everyone knows we get our bread from the supermarket. Hence, I am aware, as with so much of what I propose, that a chapter on prayer for daily bread could amount to nothing more than a spiritual pastiche. What I hope to show, however, is that to actually pray for daily bread, whether one is in urgent need of bread or not, first of all identifies the source of all provision, but also opens us up to the poor of the world and the cry for ultimate justice. In short, to pray the Lord's prayer – which is where, of course, we locate the petition for daily bread – is a daily tutoring in the Kingdom of God agenda: an abandonment of self-sufficiency and a participation in the strange world of dependency and grace.

Daily Bread in the Wilderness

The biblical origins of the prayer for daily bread are, of course, fairly easily rehearsed. In the journey through the wilderness, God tested his people by dispensing their provisions on a daily basis. In the context of a people who were used, even in their slavery, to the settled abundance of Egyptian food, the God of Israel took them through the wilderness to teach them to trust him alone for their physical needs. They were to gather only enough manna for their daily needs – no more, no less.[3] Should they gather too much, seeking to provide for the next day also, it would simply go mouldy; indeed, a friend of mine who lives in a small village in Picardy tells me that the French go to fetch bread daily for precisely the same reason, since baguettes don't last too well beyond one day![4] Thus, apart from the Sabbath eve, when they could collect two days' worth of food to cover the sacred day,[5] the basic prayer was for daily bread. And in this way God's people would stay dependent on him. For what does Western abundance do to the spirituality of a culture but sever the connection between what is on my plate and gratitude to the God who put it there in the first place? As a result of the wilderness experience, ingrained upon the psyche of God's people was the revelation that it is God who provides for our needs and that the only way to know this is to live in daily dependence on his grace:

'At twilight you will eat bread and in the morning you will be filled with bread. Then you will know that I am the Lord your God.'[6] Thus the prayer, 'Give us today our daily bread,' found its first utterance in the wilderness journey, as the people of God left the prodigious leeks and cucumbers of Egypt for the gracious, if somewhat strange, daily manna from heaven. Praying for daily bread becomes one of the ways in which the Lord keeps us close: 'Give me neither poverty nor riches, but give me only my daily bread. Otherwise I may have too much and disown you, and say "Who is the Lord?" Or I may become poor and steal and so dishonour the name of my God.'[7]

In one sense, poverty and riches are indeed relative, depending on context; like the Eton schoolboy who wrote at the beginning of his essay on poverty: 'The Father was poor; the Mother was poor. Even the Butler was poor.' What we can say, however, is that this piece of proverbial wisdom about wealth and spiritual amnesia explains why Western capitalist societies are so tough in terms of Christian mission. Churches in the south-east of England, for instance, consistently flounder, not so much on the back of widespread sexual immorality – although this is indeed a problem – as on the back of the widespread prosperity. After all, if we have all we want and much more besides, who needs God? Forgetting God is precisely what happens: as prosperity increases, so our hunger for God decreases. As Jesus warned, 'You cannot serve both God and Mammon.'[8]

So even though my own assignment to Guildford may look very attractive and may seem a cushy pastoral number, as my friends often jibe, what the virus of 'affluenza' has done is to subtly neuter the core of all true Christian spirituality which is, basic as it sounds, daily petition.[9] Once daily petition, or at the very least daily thanksgiving, for something as basic as bread is no longer necessary then little else of the revelation really makes sense. If Christian discipleship is forged on the anvil of daily dependence; prosperity has the ability of reducing it to dead nominality. If an attitude of gratitude is almost a definition of what it is to be a professing Christian, then the accumulation of wealth has the potential of robbing us of the joy of seeing God's blessing in anything less, or anything other, than material prosperity. The purity of wilderness faith, the memory of which the prophets appealed to,[10] has at its heart the crude but basic petition for bread; take that prayer away and you are left with the Laodicean conundrum of a church that is rich but is in fact wretched, pitiful, poor, blind, and naked.[11]

Thus Guildford, as an emblem of the south-east, is one of the most difficult places to thrive as a Christian. It may thrive in terms of church growth, for it rests pretty much near the centre of the Bible belt. But in terms of the Kingdom of God it struggles, precisely because material prosperity has the ability to neuter Christian discipleship. This is not to say that discipleship cannot exist. A raw faith that trusts God for the essentials is indeed possible in such a context. Living by faith is not simply the preserve of missionaries. Even so, suburbia has a propensity to strangle faith before it has even had a chance to emerge.

Conversely, some of the most vital faith you will ever encounter is found in the two-thirds world where the prayer for daily bread still means something. When you have to pray each day for food to come on the table, as the Odame family had to during the political and economic crisis of the early eighties in Ghana, it kind of does something to your faith. There were some days, my friend Mary Odame recounts, when you literally didn't know where your next meal was coming from. Every day she would pray to the Lord for food for her six young children, as well as the many members of the congregation who would turn up at the house throughout the day. This is the same woman, by the way, who on her first visit to England was taken around the supermarket and broke down in tears as she walked down the aisles of pet food. The injustice and inequality of it all was too much for her to bear. 'Your dogs eat better than us,' she exclaimed, reminding us that we must never romanticise poverty. Somewhere, however, in the mix of economic uncertainty, prayerful expectancy and daily provision, spiritual giants emerge, like Mary, who show the rest of us what it is to live with faith and gratitude.

The Real Social Gospel

How Christians in the West can recover this kind of faith is difficult to imagine. Short of an economic downturn, consumerism is so deeply rooted in our habits that it has become the primary way we define ourselves and our relationships to one another.[12] We live in a culture where wants have been turned into needs. Our young people tell us that they need a certain brand of trainer in order to stay cool (when, in the language of Monty Python, 'we were lucky even to have a pair of trainers!'). In a similar vein, our material expectations around Christmas have become so huge that the message of Christ's birth, even within Christian communities, has been almost entirely overtaken by the hype of the advertising people and the call of the High Street.

One way out of the economic challenges posed by the petition for daily bread – not to mention the economic thrust of the Lord's prayer as a whole – is to spiritualise the prayer and see daily bread simply as the word of God. There are numerous commentaries that do precisely this, and legitimately – Jesus himself in the wilderness temptations reminds us from Deuteronomy that 'Man does not live on bread alone but by every word that comes from the mouth of God.'[13] There is a strong tradition within Scripture itself of equating daily bread with the word of God. Even so, biblical spirituality is far too earthy to allow us to get away with a solely devotional approach. Praying for daily bread is unavoidably gutsy. Furthermore, praying for daily bread inevitably raises very basic questions of equality. As Paul puts it in encouraging the Christians in Corinth to give to the poor in Jerusalem, 'Our desire is not that others might be relieved while you are hard pressed but that there might be equality. At the present time your plenty will supply what they need, so that in turn their plenty will supply what you need. Then there will be equality.'[14] These were the conditions that existed in the wilderness. In the context of the daily provision of manna in the morning, appearing like thin flakes of frost, each one was to gather as much as they needed, amounting to an omer per person. And in this way, 'He who gathered much did not have too much, and he who gathered little did not have too little.'[15]

If one is to be true to the wilderness tradition therefore – and in particular to a life of daily dependence – we must, as a Christian virtue, think socially and globally. Praying the Lord's prayer as a daily discipline is a potentially subversive activity. This is no pious miscellany, but a political and economic re-reading of the present situation in which praying for daily bread is of a piece with the declaration that Christ is Lord. For those who as children prayed the Lord's prayer by rote every morning at school assembly, this comes as a huge surprise. For the earliest Christians to pray the Lord's prayer was politically dangerous; hence, it was handed on to catechumens only towards the end of the journey of initiation. By the time we get to pray 'Give us today our daily bread,' we have already prayed for the Kingdom of God to come on earth, as it is in heaven, and for the hallowing of God's name over all. Furthermore, depending on how political you want to get, the prayer to forgive others their debts as we ourselves have been forgiven, may well be a cry for release from actual financial debts, such is the sheer earthiness of the language used.[16] It cannot be that our daily lives are untouched by issues of poverty and injustice. Though we cannot save the world, to retreat into the private world of Christian piety is a terrible reduction of economically charged praying into the tame language of penitential piety. 'Give us today our daily bread' brings global economies into our prayer closets.

Far from changing the pure evangelical faith into some vague liberal gospel, being attentive to issues of economic injustice on a daily basis lies at the very heart of Christian mission. Put it like this: what kind of evangelical faith would we be talking about that could rest comfortably with the fact that millions of stomachs go hungry each day as we in the West grow fat? Being concerned about that is not evangelicals diluting their faith by espousing a social gospel. This is evangelicals echoing the heart of the prophets. As far as Ezekiel was concerned, the sins of Sodom and Gomorrah had far more to do with a surfeit of food than with homosexuality.[17] As Ray Bakke quipped to someone who had charged him with espousing a social gospel, but who also admitted to all the trappings of material prosperity: 'It seems to me that you are the one living out the social gospel.'[18] Having the latest model Lexus, insisting on two holidays a year, paying for our children's education, is about as good a definition of a social gospel as anything you will hear from the so-called radical left. In such a context, which is unmistakably Western, maybe to pray 'Give us today our daily bread' is in fact to pray 'Give us the grace to know when enough is enough' or 'Help us to say "No" when the world entices us with so much.'[19] Indeed to pray the Lord's prayer is to allow oneself to be educated daily in what is essential and what it superfluous; it is to eschew the fantasy world of the advertisers and choose to live contentedly with what we have;[20] it is tantamount to seeking first the Kingdom, trusting that as we do so, all these other things will be given to us as well.

Attacking Consumerism

For many of the above reasons, as a pastor of a suburban church I am personally committed to encouraging as many young people as I can to visit the two-thirds world early on in their lives so that they incorporate in their own prayers for daily bread the needs of the poor that they have encountered first hand. Poverty is not something that exists only in Africa. I realise that. I can walk five minutes from my house and experience it in the lives of people very much known to me. But since there is every chance in Western consumerist culture for a person to become entrenched by mid-life, embroiled in all kinds of financial commitments and material aspirations, then it seems to me, somewhat naïvely perhaps, that enabling our children to witness early on how others live could prove one of the best investments we make.

This is not without its problems, to be sure. Flying out to a place like Peru to spend three weeks on a project in a local community and then returning back to England raises more questions than it can answer, and in some ways perpetuates the problem rather than solves it. Much the same charge can be levelled against events like Live Aid. But these concerns notwithstanding, I have also seen lives completely overturned by a brief exposure to the problem of global poverty.

Consumerism, however, is more insidious than the simple demarcation between the haves and the have nots (or, as I heard recently, the yachts and the yacht-nots). Consumerism is a way of looking at life itself, and infiltrates everything down to the very way we interact with one another. In consumerist notions of exchange, to speak technically for a moment, even the way we take our leisure means we need to get something out of it. Hence, one of the other most important things that parents can do as they bring up their children, alongside raising global awareness, is to subvert the insidious effects of consumerism with real practical alternatives.

Without wanting to sound too vague, this will clearly mean different things for different people. For my wife and I it has meant doing away with the television (a decision which we regularly review with our children); but you try suggesting that in a sermon point as a way forward, which I do just for fun once a year, and you may as well commit preacher suicide. I get more comments about that sermon than just about anything else I preach on throughout the year. My idea, however, is that by doing away with the television, at least part of the year, you go straight to the source. Not only is television a poor educator,[21] but it is responsible for a great deal of the discontentedness that consumerism fosters. Furthermore, speaking as someone who grew up with TV, and had more than his fair share of dinners around the box, TV prevents what is going to prove absolutely critical to the survival of a Christian civilisation, namely what the philosopher Albert Borgmann calls 'the culture of the table'.[22]

It would perhaps be too strong to suggest that the recovery of meal times is the lynchpin upon which Western civilisation depends. Even to put it like that sounds laughable. As if cultural renewal depended on eating together. And yet, if we are to truly enter into the rhythm of a daily spirituality, learning to live eucharistically, so to speak – content with what we have and mindful of the poor – then it seems to me the meal table is about as good a place to start as any. As Capon says in his inimitable way: 'I usually say that you need only two things, two pieces of matter, to make a home: a bed and a table.'[23] It is here, around the table, in the company of friends and family and a good meal that we begin to distinguish between the hurriedness of an insatiable consumerism and the richness of leisurely conversation. In the setting of an ordinary, daily, meal time, it is possible to pause long enough in order to finally recognise – as Paul says to Timothy, echoing Genesis 1 – that in the end 'everything God created is good, and nothing is to be rejected if it is received with thanksgiving.'[24]

There will always be the super-spiritual among us who despise these ordinary gestures of food and drink. But for us who truly believe in the incarnation, a meal around a table, if taken seriously, is an intimation of a much bigger world – one that transcends the blandness of fast-food culture and hurried conversation simply by giving thanks. In the midst of the storm on the boat, surrounded by hungry men, Paul's fourfold action of taking bread, giving thanks, breaking it, and sharing it becomes a sign of God's favour to them,[25] just as Jesus' blessing over the bread in the dim evening light in Emmaus becomes a window to a couple of jaded disciples to the wonderful world of resurrection.[26] After all, what was the first thing Jesus did after he appeared to the disciples in Galilee, but cook them a breakfast?[27] Even though we might be forgiven for expecting something a little more sensational, it was our Lord's wisdom to root his resurrection in something as ordinary and as daily as a good breakfast. The daily ritual of eating breakfast together, it appears, is one of those 'signals of transcendence', as Peter Berger calls these human gestures:[28] part of a much bigger canvas than our culture has hitherto told us, upon which the stories of our lives are painted. As a rearguard action, the recovery of 'the culture of the table' will be as important as anything else Christian communities will attempt. Hospitality, in whatever shape or form, will be absolutely critical to the survival of faith in the new Dark Ages. As Peterson warns us: 'A culture of inhospitality forbodes resurrection famine.'[29]

Again, the chances of this happening are slim. Critiquing the breakfast habits of modern-day commuters, Joe Moran observes the following:

> On your way to the railway station, you just have time to nip into Starbucks or Pret à Manger to buy a 'Rise and Shine' muffin, an egg and tomato breakfast baguette, or a 'Very Berry Breakfast Bowl' (spoon supplied); a cappuccino in a polystyrene cup with a corrugated cardboard sleeve to protect your hand from the heat; and a dinky little smoothie bottle from the neatly stacked shelf in the chiller cabinet. All this will cost you your daily salary, but it has given you an extra five minutes in bed, and sold you a sense of yourself as a thoroughly modern, busy professional.[30]

Moran goes on to lament the loss not only of the English cooked breakfast but of lunch and dinner as well. Things like the rise of television, the impact of e-mail, and the sheer busyness of the workplace have done away with the whole host of these daily rituals by which our lives were enriched. But not only does the culture of busyness work against the ritual of the table; the culture of the church itself seems opposed to this kind of simplicity. As with so many sacramental gestures – such as baptism, eucharist, confession – it seems to me that we Christians, nonconformists in particular, fall between two stools when it comes to something like a meal. We feel sure it has something to do with Jesus. He clearly wasn't called 'a glutton and a drunkard' for nothing (whatever else we know about the historical Jesus, one thing even the Jesus seminar people agree upon is that he ate with tax collectors and sinners). But we are not well practised enough with the culture of the table to know how to fully enter it. Hence, the grace that is said prior to the meal is something of an apology, if not an embarrassment – that is, if it is said at all – and the meal, if we are not careful, descends once more into hurriedness.

If the slow movement has anything to say to us, it started off by saying this: a hurried meal is a contradiction in terms. A meal is an event. It is a place where we share our lives together. One of the things we do around our own table is have everyone tell their story. In fact we have a little tradition in my own home where around the table all the people, adults and children, will be asked, in a light-hearted way, to grade their day out of ten, and in this way bare something of their soul.

For those who are guests around our table, it seems rather quaint to do such a thing, if somewhat cute as well; but actually what is happening is crucially important, for it affirms the utter uniqueness and wonder of each person there, simply for being there at the table. You are what you eat; or more poignantly, you are who you eat with. A companion is someone, by definition, who you share bread with – *cum* (with) *panis* (bread). There is nothing utilitarian about it. Actually, lingering around the meal table could be regarded as a classic waste of time. But who cares? What the table recovers, and what hospitality in general makes possible, is the wonder and the mystery of this one person. As we give thanks to God for providing our daily bread, suddenly the table is transformed from a regular meal into a heavenly banquet where everyone is viewed with different lenses. The food doesn't change; a simple meal doesn't suddenly become cordon bleu. At least I have never seen that happen. But the occasion changes. God transforms even the most ordinary meal into a right royal feast.

The Supper of the Lamb

I don't read a lot of books on church growth. I am weary of looking at the world through the eyes of statisticians. I think the church can do better than this. Instead of thinking about grand strategies to win people for Christ, I reckon simply recovering this kind of table fellowship would be enough. Moreover it would help, like it did with Jesus, to break down the barriers of race, ethnicity, gender, and age, by recognising the equality and significance of each person around the table. In seeking to express a vision in our own church of being a community where there is 'neither Jew nor Greek, male nor female, slave nor free, but all are one,'[31] eating together in large community gatherings has been central to making that happen. Having people around the table from Africa or China, as often happens in our church, certainly does something to your understanding of the body of Christ. It brings the world to our table, enriches our community, and for those of us who are hosts, puts names and faces on the petition 'Give us today our daily bread.'

It is worth noting– as we bring this chapter to a close – that exegetically there is some debate over the wording of Matthew's text. Whereas Luke says 'give us our bread day by day', Matthew uses a very unusual word, *epiousios*, leading some commentators to translate it, 'give us the bread of tomorrow'. It is a possible alternative translation for the more common 'daily bread'. Either way, however, it amounts to the same thing. Whether it is praying for daily bread or the bread of tomorrow, both translations give expression to a basic prayer of trust that God will provide, and therefore I need not be anxious.[32]

What is more intriguing is whether this Greek word *epiousios* has more eschatological overtones: that is, Jesus is telling us to pray not simply for our daily bread, but for the bread of the coming day, meaning the bread that belongs to the glorious future of the heavenly banquet, when justice and righteousness are established and Christ will illuminate the world.[33] In a possible allusion to the practice of gathering twice as much on the Sabbath eve, is not the prayer for the next day's bread a prayer for Sabbath bread, a prayer for that day when the creation will know the Sabbath rest? Though we have no exegetical grounds to say this is definitely what Jesus means, it seems consistent with the already/not yet tension of New Testament theology to speculate a little that this dimension would be in Jesus' mind. To pray the Lord's prayer – Thy Kingdom come, Thy will be done, Give us today our daily bread – is not only to pray for present needs, but to do so in anticipation of the coming kingdom and the coming day when these petitions will be fully realised at the heavenly banquet. Trusting in God for one's daily needs, giving to the needs of the poor, gathering people around the table, breaking bread together in our homes, the eucharistic meal itself – these are not simply things done in a theological vacuum, but intimations in and of themselves of that great day when we will eat together at the Lord's banquet. To gather friends together around the table and to eat together is both an echo of the resurrection, when Jesus ate breakfast with his disciples, and a foretaste of the consummation.

8

The Lord's Day

I was in the Spirit on the Lord's Day.[1]

Sunday 11 January
This morning I started making a new comic called Crunch. I have done three
pages already. This afternoon we went down to Nanny Collins and I got my
Monster Fun. We all looked at Nan's old photos. We watched The Prince
and the Pauper *and* Holiday '76 *and they showed you a holiday in*
Scotland. After tea me and Simon played Subbuteo *and the score was 0-0.*
Then we watched World About Us *about insects and we went up to bed and*
I ordered my Scoop book (Ice Cold in Alex) and I got my dinner money
ready.[2]

A few years ago the journalist Andrew Collins wrote a memoir of
growing up in the seventies entitled *Where Did it All Go Right?*
Like my own seventies childhood it was idyllic in many ways,
but totally devoid of church. In fact, we were so secularised we
didn't even go to church at Christmas or Easter. About the clos-
est my friends and I got to a Christian liturgy, I recollect, was the
annual Harvest Festival at the local Anglican church.

That said, in seventies Britain Sunday was still a decidedly different day. Even for non-churchgoers like ourselves, I remember
it as a quieter day – less traffic for sure. And though social mobility was already at work in splitting up extended families, my
grandma would invariably visit for Sunday lunch. Those were
the days when you knew where you were: all football matches
kicked off at three o'clock on a Saturday afternoon, so by Sunday
morning you had a complete up-to-date league table – at least
until the mid-seventies, when Sunday fixtures started to mess

things up. My abiding memories relate to the Sunday evening ritual of my mother washing my hair with Vosene shampoo, the
smell of which I can still invoke at will, even now.

For me, therefore, as is the case for many people who have
grown up outside the Christian community, Christian conversion
had a direct and immediate impact on what I did on a Sunday
and, by implication, on the shape of the rest of the week. Instead
of Sunday as the archetypical anti-climax of the secular weekend,
with the accompanying last rites of getting one's things ready for
Monday morning, quite suddenly it was transfigured into the
first day of the week, and the day I looked forward to most. To be
honest, this was due in part to the fact that the church I attended
had a very lively Sunday evening service. Furthermore it seemed
to me that just about every young girl in town went there. For a
seventeen-year-old boy, as I am sure you can imagine, that was a
pretty powerful incentive for regular churchgoing. Sunday really
was special. It had been redeemed, even as I had been redeemed.

These days, however, Lord's Day worship simply does not
have the pull that it once had over the Christian community.
Once upon a time a 'Twicer' was someone who attended church
both Sunday morning and Sunday evening; it was both a virtue
and a burden (I certainly don't insist that people at Millmead
must come to both services). These days, however, the term
'Twicer' describes the more casual approach to churchgoing for
many Christians: namely twice a month.

Such scant regard for Sunday is justified by recourse to the
old argument that Christianity is more than just church attendance. To use Sunday attendance as a yardstick by which to
judge the spiritual maturity of a congregation, so it is argued, is
to reduce life in the Spirit to narrow institutional forms and to
be guilty of cultural irrelevance. Maybe so; I have had to get
delivered myself from the kind of spirituality that measures
everything by Sunday attendance. But at a time when our culture has all but obliterated the spiritual significance of Sunday
as a day that is different, let alone a day of worship, I would like
to offer a counter-argument: that for Christians to take Sunday
seriously in our day could indeed be a radical restatement of
what it means to confess Jesus Christ as Lord. In this chapter I
would like to explore this idea, for if Christians are to live a day

well then it seems to me important that we understand the significance of this, their own, day.

'We cannot be without the *dominicum*'

> And on the day they called Sunday, all who live in cities or in the country gather to one place, and the memories of the apostles or the writings of the prophets are read, as long as time permits; then when the reader has ceased, the president verbally instructs, and exhorts to the imitation of these good things. Then we all rise together and pray, and, as we before said, when our prayer is ended, bread and wine and water are brought, and the president in like manner offers prayers and thanksgivings, according to his ability, and the people assent saying Amen.[3]

There is no doubt about it: those who knock Sunday worship as a relic from our ecclesiastical past are on to something. As has been stated elsewhere, with reference to Sabbath, the conflation of Sunday and Sabbath rest arose from the Christendom project. It was Constantine, the first Roman emperor to become a Christian, who commanded his subjects to rest on Sunday in 321 AD, and from that time onwards the day was protected in many Christian nations by legislation.

Even so, for all the associations of Sunday worship with civic religion, the desire to recover Lord's Day worship should not be dismissed as simply a wistful longing for a lost Christendom. That would be guilty of the kind of naïve historicism people like Dan Brown ply: in *The Da Vinci Code* he seems to want to trace every major theological doctrine and practice of the church to Constantine's conversion. However, as our above quotation from Justin Martyr demonstrates, Lord's Day worship took place among Christian communities from the earliest times, and can even be traced back to the New Testament.[4] It was, after all, the Lord's Day, when Christians remembered the resurrection of Christ and, as Roger Beckwith and Wilfred Stott have sought to demonstrate, may have even incorporated elements of the Jewish Sabbath.[5]

From these New Testament roots, the early church Fathers reflected a great deal on the importance of Sunday worship for

Christian communities in a pagan culture. In what is probably the earliest and most important post-biblical epistle, the *Didache*, we find reference to 'The Lord's (Day) of the Lord,'[6] and what is meant by this is not the apocalyptic Day of the Lord, but Sunday worship, or what soon became known as the *dominicum*. As Gordon Lathrop points out, 'This assembly is inextricably linked to Christian identity. When certain Christians of North Africa in the early fourth century were accused of illegally gathering, they made a confession that contributed to their martyrdom: "We cannot be without the *dominicum*." They meant not that they could not do without the day, but that they could not be Christians or even live in any real sense without the assembly and its content, the risen Lord.'[7] If this is in any way correct as history, then such devotion to the Lord's Day acts as something of a rebuke to modern-day Christians who, facing a not dissimilar pagan culture, seem to have drifted with the tide of secularism regarding Sunday, and often don't gather for weeks on end.

Not that I am advocating a 'Keep Sunday Special' campaign; that would be Constantianism. In my opinion, we Christians need to be careful when it comes to legislating for the world. Often we end up confusing the roles of church and state. But when it comes to our own sense of Christian identity, we likewise ought to be careful not to let the world legislate for us. One of the reasons why Lord's Day worship was so significant for the earliest Christians was because, in addition to acting as a memorial to the Lord, it acted as the vanguard to a new world. In terms that are deeply eschatological, it is the Day of the Lord: the pivot of history when the future comes rushing into the present in the resurrection of Christ. In that sense every Sunday is Easter Sunday, when the world of the future breaks into time and space – or, as Sunday was increasingly referred to, the eighth day of creation.[8] As Lathrop puts it, 'The observance of the week and the meeting of the eighth day: this juxtaposition, understood in the manner of the biblical rhetoric that uses the old in speaking the new, is the *ordo* of the church. It provides a patterning for Christian ritual, and at the same time it bears the deepest faith of the church and forms us in that faith.'[9]

Counter-cultural Witness

My hope in giving this brief survey of the history surrounding the theology of Lord's Day worship is to deliver it from the notions of dead institutionalism with which its detractors have daubed it. On the contrary, in the present post-modern context, observing the Lord's Day could be a subversive act of Christian witness, and biblical to boot. Set alongside the cosy Sunday morning breakfast television with the politicians, the review of the Sunday papers, or the incessant pull of the Sunday sporting calendar, Lord's Day worship acts as a powerful counter-claim to these secular idols, restating the grand narrative of a world in which Christ is Lord.[10] As Rodney Clapp puts it: 'However feebly or distractedly we participate, we are acknowledging a reality outside ourselves and the world as it is otherwise known. We are confessing at least the possibility of being accountable to something (to someone) other than our individual desires and "needs".'[11]

It is not that absence from church on Sunday is fatal to the rest of that particular week, any more than missing a morning prayer time cancels out the possibility of living a day prayerfully. As has already been stated, Christian commitment is obviously a great deal more than Sunday attendance. But in so far as worship is about centring on God, then failure to participate in Lord's Day worship on a regular basis leaves us prey to just about everything and anything. As more than one parishioner will tell you, a week without Lord's Day worship is to run the risk of living erratically. Whilst church is clearly seven days a week – Christianity played out in offices, in schools, in the home – it is especially church when it gathers on the Lord's Day. To persist with the idea that this is no more significant than Christians meeting in Starbucks, as some are now saying, is to consistently and mischievously, in my opinion, undermine the given means of grace through which Christ embraces his church; it is to misunderstand the importance of ritual in our lives – whatever our spiritual tradition – and remove a vital component of spiritual formation, if not the most important component. Why do churches spend so much time and money on those who preach and lead worship? It's not necessarily a case of blind devotion to one way of being church. In my experience these churches know full well that the ministry of the church extends well beyond the gathering of the church, and they say so in their annual budgets. But the reason so much energy is devoted to what happens on the Lord's Day is because these same churches know that the wider ministry of the church hinges on the distinctively Christian kind of shaping that takes place in gatherings of the people of God. Lord's Day worship is crucial, in every sense of the word. It is central to the formation of a people.[12]

So fundamental is Lord's Day worship to Christian witness that even the gospel narratives are framed in the setting of the worshipping community. For those of us who like to take our scriptures neat, this statement may seem somewhat outrageous. A commitment to *sola scriptura,* which many evangelicals espouse – in theory if not in practice – means that it is almost impossible to acknowledge the presence of liturgical patterns within the Bible. Yet, liturgical shapes there undoubtedly are, and never more so than in the resurrection narratives, where there is clear evidence of the narrative being reworked to reflect the worshipping life of the church. If Mary Magdalene went to the tomb of Jesus at the earliest possible opportunity after the Sabbath, Luke wants us to know that this was 'Early on the first day of the week.'[13] That is to say: the first day of the week, or the eighth day, when the Christians gather, is the day of Christ's resurrection.

In a very real sense, coming hard on the back of the seventh day, this resurrection day is like unto the first day of a new creation: a day in the midst of an ordinary week when the church encounters the Risen Lord himself, and thus bears witness to his new creation. Why else does Luke tell the Emmaus road story in the way he does? Obviously Luke is a historian. This episode on the road to Emmaus really did happen: Jesus really did open up the scriptures to these two bewildered disciples, and he really did become the host on that first Easter evening; taking bread, giving thanks, breaking it, and giving it to them. Luke is recording it for his most excellent friend Theophilus. However, Luke also wants us to spot the ecclesial connections: in the opening up of the scriptures, on the first day of the week, hearts really are set on fire; and in the breaking of bread Jesus really is recognised. In the great reversal of the fall, 'their eyes were opened and they recognised him'.[14] In fact very quickly after Pentecost it is no wonder that the followers of Jesus 'devoted themselves to the apostles' teaching and to the fellowship, to the breaking of bread and to prayer,'[15] for it was here that they encountered the Risen Christ.

Attending to the Real World

It hardly needs to be said that regular churchgoing is not without its problems. After all, when you think about it, going to church every Sunday is a little strange. Where else these days do you participate in community singing? Where else do you hear a monologue of over half an hour? One lady in my last church used to time my sermons by the number of Extra Strong Mints she could get through. Though it offended me at first, finally I suggested she submit it to the publishers of one of those '101 things to do during a sermon' books. It never bothered me after that. What bothered me more was the often-heard quip at the end of the service, often as the person is leaving the building and shaking the minister's hand: 'Well, I guess it is back to the real world.' As if what they had been doing for the last hour and a half was totally irrelevant to the rest of the week.

Given the content of what we offer on certain Sundays, maybe they were justified in their remark. But my suspicion is that people who say these things are not commenting about a particular Sunday, but about the notion of Sunday worship itself: that to go to church on a Sunday is to escape to an unreal world which, although it may be a pleasant distraction, is not really where the action is.

But how about a different way of looking at this? How about turning the whole thing upside down and imagining that in churchgoing we enter the real – if somewhat unfamiliar – country of grace and salvation, from which we re-enter the unreal world with fresh eyes? As Heschel so typically puts it: 'Worship is a way of seeing the world in the light of God.'[16] Or at least that is what ought to happen. Through exposure to the hearing of scripture, God-honouring singing, prayers of intercession, baptismal obedience, and the breaking of bread, we orientate ourselves to a different world than the one we have come from in the week, in order to judge that same world and more importantly ourselves through the lens of church. Through these ordinary churchly gestures, we get delivered from the world of impersonal statistics, league table obsession and target-driven living, into a world where we are named, blessed and affirmed. Regular participation in Lord's Day worship makes possible the transformation of an 'I–it' world into an 'I–thou' world.[17]

It doesn't always seem like that at the time. For many of us church is frighteningly bland. These ordinary gestures seem precisely that: dull liturgies that change no one. But what John is telling us in Revelation is that even the most poorly attended congregation and even the dullest service has this apocalyptic promise. 'St John's vision shows his congregations that what they are presently doing in worship corresponds to what presently takes place at the very heart of things, heaven.'[18] Those ropey songs we sing are part of the heavenly anthem; that interminable preaching we listen to is the living word of God; and those seemingly harmless intercessions we send up as sweet smelling perfume return back in thunder and lightning.[19]

Lord's Day worship for John is not simply religious observance but resurrection witness; and in a world of consumer idolatry the simple technique of going to church is about as subversive as you can get. The gathering of the church on the first day of the week is nothing less than a foretaste of the great heavenly banquet; a rehearsal of the great Day of the Lord; a participation in the actual worship of heaven. Pastorally, it is like the tide coming in. As Evelyn Underhill so graphically puts its:

> Many a congregation when it assembles in church must look to the angels like a muddy puddly shore at low tide; littered with every kind of rubbish and odds and ends – a distressing sort of spectacle. And then the tide of worship comes in, and it's all gone, the dead sea urchins and jellyfish, the paper and the empty cans and the nameless bits of rubbish. The cleansing sea flows over the whole lot. So we are released from a narrow selfish outlook on the universe by a common act of worship.[20]

From Mount Zion to Mount Carmel

Again, Sunday worship can be anything but this. Sometimes it conforms to the aspirations of the very world we have just come from. The two-hour slot or so that we give to worship on a Sunday can be just as manic as anything else we do the rest of the week. Instead of providing a counter-liturgy by which to judge the world's hurriedness, contemporary worship too easily succumbs to an anxiety-driven rhythm of its own. Far from reconceiving the world through the daybreak colours of the new creation, our worship can at times simply mimic the restlessness of the world we have come from, leaving us as exhausted as when we came in.

This is not a plea for quieter worship, or the removal of drums. That is beside the point. There is nothing inherently more spiritual about contemplative worship over against a more Pentecostal style of worship, and those who suggest there is are guilty of spiritual snobbery. The issue is theology. Whether it is a hymn sandwich or alternative worship, once worship is conceived out of a desire to have a worship experience, or even as a way of placating the traditionalists, then, theologically speaking, it ceases to be worship. At worst, in my neck of the woods, it ends up as Baalism. As worshippers gather together, seeking by their efforts to get somewhere, we subtly move from Mount Zion with thousands of angels in joyful assembly, the church of the firstborn, and Jesus Christ, the mediator of a new covenant,[21] to Mount Carmel and the prophets of Baal, seeking to induce the presence of God by their sword slashing. Indeed, on more occasions than I care to remember, this is exactly what Lord's Day worship became in some churches I have known. It got pretty close to someone actually drawing blood, as the worship leader sought to drum up God's presence. Though it looked and sounded impressive, it amounted to nothing less than a denial of Christ's victory. Such worship acts as if the resurrection has never taken place, and as such will inevitably end up as classic gnosticism.[22] For if the resurrection of Christ is the reaffirmation of God's creation, then worship that is devoid of resurrection wonder will end up as a denial of our humanity and thus have no bearing whatsoever upon the rest of the week. It is worship that neither derives from where we have come, nor relates to where we are going. It is simply worship time, whatever that means.

The cultural roots of this kind of worship are not particularly hard to uncover. They lie somewhere in late sixties expressionism, coupled to an all-pervasive consumerism that is so deeply rooted in our patterns of behaviour now that we are hardly aware of it. To change the metaphor, consumerism is the air we breathe. As a pastor, and as one who is responsible for planning worship, I notice it particularly in the comments people make after services. Many of them betray a customer mentality. If it is not the worship, it is the preaching; if it is not the preaching, it is the children's talk; if it is not the children's talk, it is the heating. It seems as if consumerism is so deep, we just can't help ourselves. We arrive having already decided that if I do not get something out of the worship, then I may well just look for another church.

If Lord's Day worship is to mean anything, therefore, and make a significant contribution to the spiritual formation of the Christian community, then we will have to find ways of overcoming this kind of consumer approach to worship. Furthermore, if contemporary worship is to avoid degenerating into a kind of gnosticism, it will need to recover the basic theological tenet that all Christian worship has a certain givenness to it that is quite separate to whether we feel God's presence in worship or not. Christian worship is not dependent on the ability of a congregation to drum up the presence of the Lord, for the Lord is already here, in the Spirit, and before the Father, gathering the church around himself. It is not the worship leader who should be burdened with the responsibility of making worship happen. That way lies legalism, making Sunday into a day as exhausting as any other. Rather, Jesus is the worship leader, who week after week, gathers the congregation around himself, taking our feeble prayers and our half-baked sermons and our out-of-tune singing, bringing them to the Father as acceptable and pleasing worship. Whether we feel it or not, Lord's Day worship happens simply because the Lord wills it to happen.

Of course, there are ways of going about this. I have learnt from painful experience that deploying the word liturgy as I have done doesn't always endear you to the listener. It is like a red rag to a bull. Liturgy is what we are trying to get delivered from, they argue. But this is not quite true. Every church has a liturgy. Even those churches that claim not to have a liturgy have a liturgy. Simply deciding not to adhere to a fixed liturgy but to be open to the Spirit is in itself a form of liturgy and, ironically, is oftentimes more predictable than those churches that actually use a liturgy. So the question is not: 'Do you have a liturgy?' The question is: 'Is it a good liturgy?' Is it a liturgy that helps form us into disciples of Christ, immersing us in the grammar of faith, or is it a liturgy that fails to deliver on the basis of a limited vocabulary? Is it a liturgy that helps us make sense of the world, or is it a liturgy that encourages us to escape from the world?

Often it is the latter that prevails in our so-called contemporary worship; characterised by a strangely ahistorical kind of gospel. That is why, as Clapp points out, 'we must insist that liturgy, far from being an escape from the real world, is the real world. God is at work, in all of reality, not merely in our fleeting hours of public worship. But humanity is a blinded race, and in worship we have a chance to look on the world as it truly is – the beloved and redeemed creation of God, Father, Son and Holy Spirit.'[23] In short, the liturgy must be substantial enough for us to hear the sounds of that world; it must have enough scripture in it for the language of faith to eventually become our first language; it must have enough shape and gesture to it to ensure that the congregation experiences more than just a medley of the latest songs but a movement of grace, from the gathering rite all the way through to the benediction. Clapp is right: 'Mission is the work of the people Monday through Saturday, done after and formed by the work of the people on the first day, Sunday. Mission and witness is living every day according to the vision granted us, especially and most intensely when we gather for worship.'[24] If our liturgy is weak, our mission is weak; if our liturgy is strong, however – replete with scripture, song, intercession, preaching, and communion – Lord's Day worship takes on the significance it should do among the people of God, acting as the fulcrum to the overall worshipping life of the church.

Whether this means we should adopt the church calendar or change our church architecture is a moot point, and one that lies beyond the concerns of this chapter. My own involvement in the Deep Church conversation has led me to believe that our churchly rites need to be far more substantial than they are.[25] But to be honest, that is not really the issue. As much as I prefer, like everyone else does, a particular style of worship and a particular way of doing things, the issue at the end of the day is not style but expectation. What do we think happens when we come together on a Sunday?

For me, if someone goes away a bit confused by what has happened, a bit befuddled by the message, and a bit overwhelmed by the singing, I don't worry any more. I take it as a compliment. Somewhere in the liturgy they have encountered something that is bigger than them, that cannot be reduced to a soundbite or a slogan. What bothers me more is when people go away with everything intact; for it is likely that we have reduced our liturgy to the lowest common denominator. Sunday worship has ceased to be the strange new world of the scriptures, but the all too familiar world of the consumer.

One bold pastor who felt all these concerns decided he would take the issue by the scruff of the neck. He would go straight to the heart. Like many pastors he was tired of the way his congregation treated their Sunday worship, so he said to his congregation: 'Next week, I don't want you to come to church.' Not surprisingly his comment was met with stunned silence. Some of his congregation were mortified. What on earth would they do next Sunday? Others were overjoyed. At last, a Sunday off – a chance to be normal. But before these thoughts were allowed to develop, he added something else: 'No, I don't want you to come to church next week. I want you to gather.'

Lord's Day worship is not the Sabbath. It would be a mistake to conflate the two. The burden of the chapter on the Sabbath was not to institute Sunday rest, but to encourage a lifestyle of rest. It may well be that the coming together of worship and rest on a Sunday is particularly appropriate at this time in our cultural history. I don't have a strong view on that, one way or the other. But however these things play out in the years to come, one thing we Christians must retrieve is the sense of occasion when we meet on the Lord's Day. Whichever church you go to, 'Don't go to church next week, but gather.' Sunday is a strange day, to be sure. The Lord's Day is unlike any other. But that is precisely the point. As Lathrop so beautifully puts it:

It is as if the meeting were after the week, beyond the week, free of the week, an opening to a thing the week cannot contain. It is, as is the resurrection, 'when the Sabbath was over.' Indeed, the resurrection of Christ – beyond the world yet saving the world, the way for us to understand and live in the world – is what the meeting is always about.[26]

9

Time, Space, Rhythm, and Place

To see a World in a Grain of Sand,
And a Heaven in a Wild Flower,
Hold Infinity in the palm of your hand
And Eternity in an hour.[1]

This final chapter carries a warning. It contains words within it like existentialism and eschatology. It mentions philosophers like Søren Kierkegaard and Augustine. My hope in this concluding chapter is to draw some thoughts together and place *The Day is Yours* in a wider framework in which the practice of living a day well intersects with long-standing theological reflections on the question of time and eternity. We have been doing some of this reflection already, as we have made our way through the rhythm of the week, and the liturgy of the hours in particular. What I would like to do now is be more explicit about these connections, and thereby make the claim that living a day well by being attentive to the movements of God's Holy Spirit is to live in one of those thin places where time, space and eternity converge.

Prior to any theologising about time, we already know from the way we ourselves experience time that it is a somewhat mysterious entity. We talk about making time, quality time, managing time, losing time. Contrary to time being a fixed standard, which is what is appears to be, time is elastic. Sometimes it ponders like a snail hauling its load across the pathway; other times it is like an express train shooting through the countryside. Depending on what we are doing it can shorten and it can lengthen; it can meander and it can speed up. As Joseph O'Conner says of Eliza Mooney in his epic novel *Redemption Falls*, 'Time continued moving in ways she did not understand. A minute takes an hour on a hardscrabble road but a morning skitters by if you're resting.'[2] Or, to use more familiar phrases: 'Time flies when you're having fun,' Martin Boroson reminds us, but 'a watched pot never boils'.[3]

Why a number of us now feel compelled to write is because in the last couple of decades time has sped up at an alarming rate. Time is flying these days – not only when you are having fun but pretty much all the time. In the 24/7 world, which is now well and truly among us, time slows down for no one. Certainly in the south-east of England, where I live, time is running so fast that as Alice says to the Red Queen: 'We must keep running to stay in the same spot.'

I guess one of the reasons this has happened is because we fear stopping; we fear the ordinariness that life outside the fast lane will mean; we fear our own company. One of the reasons we need to check our e-mails so often, or text so regularly, or watch television so frequently, is because the prospect of living with ourselves is just too frightening. But the consequences of living in such a fast-paced world are now beginning to become apparent. All over the place, both inside and outside religious communities, people are waking up to the fact that such a way of living is not only unsustainable, but destructive. Whilst Africa might be poor in things but rich in time, we in the prosperous West are rich in things, but poor in time. We have lost our soul.

The answer, moreover, amounts to more than just incremental changes here and there. All that is achieved by that is a nice 'bolt on spirituality' to an otherwise frenetic life. Rather, the answer lies in a radical change of mindset – a reorientation, if you will – to a wholly different way of looking at time, out of which distinct Christian practices emerge in order to protect this time. The answer lies in the recognition that time belongs to God, not to us. As Peter writes: 'A day is like a thousand years and a thousand years are like a day.'[4] With the Lord, it is not so much the quantity of our lives that is important so much as the quality – not so much the length of our years, as the intensity of them. It is entirely possible to live a long life and never really live and, conversely, possible to live a short life and live it to the full. It all depends on who is in charge. Presuming to be masters of our destiny, time tantalises us with the realisation that there is so much that will be left undone, so much that we will never achieve – hence the rush. Confessing to the Lordship of Christ, however, time submits to us, in the knowledge that 'Better is one day in your courts than a thousand elsewhere.'[5]

It is this celebration of the day that has been my preoccupation throughout this book. Our life is a succession of 'This is the day's.' Each one is present to us. Caught between the intersection of time and God's eternity, a day in the Bible is not simply a succession of twenty-four hours on the clock, but a unique and present appointment between the beginning of God's world – its *arche* – and its end – the *eschaton*. The *this-ness* of a day, to borrow a concept of Gerard Manley Hopkins, reminds us that though the notion of a day lived well respects the schedule of our diaries, it is not reduced to that. A day is a *kairos* moment in time. If *chronos* is the time by which our ever so modern lives are determined, *kairos* is a qualitatively different notion of time: it is an opportunity, or fulfilment. Living according to this understanding of time, we are not simply watching time pass as a quantitative measure, lamenting time past, wishing time away, and waiting for the time to come. Instead, we enter what our spiritual mentors call 'the sacrament of the present moment,'[6] in which the future and indeed the past to some extent find definition in this actual moment that I am living now. This is what the Bible means by eternal life. The glorious future of our existence, when God will be all in all, has broken into the present time. Eternity does not wait for when I die and go to glory, but when I live this day well. This day carries within it an intimation of that day, and a foretaste of a world governed not by effort but by grace.[7]

The Next Day

Realistically, not every day will take on this character. Indeed, it would be a kind of tyranny itself to expect that every day could be lived with this kind of intensity. Living with the anticipation of this kind of existence would involve a self-consciousness about the meaning of life that, paradoxically, would be the death of true Christian spirituality. Any genuine Christian existence must allow for things to work out not quite as we wanted, and even for failure. We must give ourselves permission to have a bad day, without thinking that the whole of our Christian life is in jeopardy. Some days the clock does rule, pressures seem too much, and we go to bed exhausted. Given the realities of modern-day living that is all right.

Nevertheless, to live *solely* by the dictates of *chronos* time is to run the risk of missing so much. The Scottish poet Dan Paterson laments how in his life the times when he has actually lived in the 'present moment' would amount, ironically, to no more than a single day. In effect, he is lamenting the loss of each and every day. Indeed, he goes on to say that 'if only I could have lived it as a single day; it would have thrown its light on to all the others, like a brazier in a dark arcade. Instead I find my way by sparks and what they briefly make visible.'[8] And maybe this is all that is possible in this life. Maybe our project of living each day to the maximum is too ambitious, too indulgent even. Maybe life simply needs to happen, after which, and only after which, can we make any sense of it. There is something in that idea for sure. But, returning to the wisdom of Jesus, there is most definitely something about staving off the prospect of the many days ahead and giving ourselves solely to the prospect and the possibilities of the day that presents itself to me now.

By living this way, maybe we are doing what Paul exhorts Timothy to do, which is to 'Take hold of the eternal life to which you were called.'[9] Since Christian existence is, by definition, a fulfilment of the age to come,[10] and since today is the only day we can actually live out that life of the Spirit, then in a sense living one day at a time is to enter into the 'life that is truly life'.[11] It is to transcend time that is merely linear, in which we worry about the future, into time that is aeonic, where the future breaks into the present.[12]

Kierkegaard wrote of our need 'to cram today with eternity and not with the next day', and wondering how Jesus lived 'without anxiety', believes it is because 'he had eternity with him in the day that is called today, and therefore the next day had no power over him, it had no existence for him'.[13] Thus, not only are we presented with the gift of today, but every today intensifies into the gift of each and every moment. And to be present, so to speak, in each and every moment, is to redeem time and taste life that is truly life.

It doesn't have to be anything particularly sensational in order for it to constitute life. It might be something as simple as a meal around the table, taking the children to school, or travelling on the train to London. The essence of Christian spirituality is not escape into some heightened spiritual atmosphere, but embracing the real and the ordinary. Again, Kierkegaard has an interesting take on this in *Fear and Trembling* in the figure of the knight who has learnt to transcend the distractedness of temporal life by living in the intensity of the eternal. This does not make him a mystic (although it may make him an existentialist), because this knight has his feet planted firmly on the ground. In fact, by all outward appearances you would not know he was any different from the rest of humanity. Kierkegaard has him tending to his work, going to church, walking in the forest, passing the time of day with a friend, walking home of an evening to his wife and the meal she has prepared for him. To look at him in the evening smoking his pipe, notes Kierkegaard, 'one would swear that it was the grocer over the way vegetating in the twilight'. He is no different. And yet, 'this man has made and every instant is making the movements of infinity'.[14] He lives with passion. He lives with faith. Without this intensity, this concentration of thought in one act of consciousness, a man will never come to the point of making this movement, he argues.

What Kierkegaard is referring to is the leap and life of faith. To live beyond the sensibilities of civic religion one must live with a deep internal and existential sense of things believed. One must live intensely in the here and now, and not worry about tomorrow. In *Christian Discourses* Kierkegaard explains that: 'The next day – it is the grappling-hook by which the prodigious hulk of anxiety gets a hold of the individual's light craft. If it succeeds, he is under the dominion of that power. The next day is the first link of the chain that fetters a person to that superfluous anxiety that is of the evil one.'[15]

In Praise of Slow Spirituality

For a culture that is living in the fast track, and seeking to lay hold of the future, I appreciate that all of this sounds rather pedestrian. In a country like North America which is still striving in its politics for that manifest destiny, a spirituality that seeks to slow things down a bit seems positively weak. In fact, the one thing our consumerist culture fears above all else is the prospect that our years might be cut short and that we will never achieve what we purposed to do in life. Hence the hurriedness of modern life; hence the desperate attempts to stay young; hence, the huge anxiety that has now lodged in the stomach of our everyday existence. But as Moltmann argues, as he himself comes to the latter part of his life, and reflects on concepts of time and eternity,

> It is not length of life in terms of time which reaches out to the originality which when we think of God we call eternity. It is the depth of experience in the moment. Chronological time has nothing to do with this eternity of God's. But the fulfilled moment is like an atom of eternity, and its illumination is like a spark of the eternal light.[16]

Moltmann calls this concept of time aeonic time. It is heavenly time that breaks into the present, investing each day with its richness, impregnating even the most ordinary routine activities with depth of meaning. And it is precisely this concept of present-ness that allows Moltmann to celebrate what our culture is increasingly eroding in the name of economic productivity: namely childhood. After all, if eternal life is about embracing the present-ness of this day, then childhood ceases to be simply a preparation stage for adult life, but a state of existence to be enjoyed in and of itself. Indeed, every stage of life can be embraced in this way: as a gift to be received in all its uniqueness and particularity. Rather than going through life lamenting time past, or wishing time would move on, we can immerse ourselves in the season of our life as that which is unique to me now. We can embrace eternal life by the simple act of thanking God for the day I have now.

For Moltmann this convergence of eternity and the present time is tied to the natural cycles of time. The cycles of day and night, summer and winter, carry intimations of a world without end, life in a permanent mode of duration.[17] Thus, without wanting to deify the natural cycles of the world – which is not what is going on in biblical spirituality – we are back with our notion of each and every new morning as a kind of sacrament of God's eternal grace: 'Because of the Lord's great love we are not consumed, for his compassions never fail. They are new every morning.'[18] In that sense, as Augustine mused in *De Genesi ad Litteram*, we are always in day one of creation. In his exegesis of the biblical text, Augustine came to see that since all God's work was done as soon as he said 'Let there be light,' then in effect he created in one day only; each new day is the prolongation of God's eternity that found expression in that first day. Thus, he argues in *The Confessions*,

> Your years abide together at once, because they abide. They do not pass away when new ones arrive and cut them off, for they do not pass away; whereas our years will all be when they will all not exist. *Your years are but one day* (Ps. 90:4 [Ps. 89:4], 2 Pet. 3:8), and your day is not 'every day' but 'today', since your today does not give way to your tomorrow, nor take over from your yesterday. Your today is eternity; therefore him to whom you said *Today I have begotten you* (Ps. 2:7; Acts 13:33, Heb. 1:5; 5:5), you begat as your coeternal. You are the one who have made all times, and who are before all times, nor at any time was there not time.[19]

It sounds weird. It sounds like Bill Murray's *Groundhog Day*: we wake up at 6 o'clock on 2 February only to discover that we have been here before.[20] But that is not what we mean. To say that we are always in day one of creation is not to imagine that we are trapped in a continual replay. Rather, to live in day one is to wake up with the knowledge that this new day is infused with that same Genesis light that exploded onto the world by divine fiat: 'Morning has broken, like the first morning.'[21] It is to live in the eternal today of God's time. As the writer to the Hebrews exhorts his congregation, 'Today, if you hear his voice, do not harden your hearts.'[22] In contrast to the wilderness generation, lamented in Psalm 95, where for forty years the people of God tested and tried the Lord, we are called to break that meandering disobedience by the simple act of living today. Outlandish as it may sound, the mystery of eternity is wrapped up in daily attentiveness. Communion with God is affirmed by the way we embrace this one day. As I open myself up to the uniqueness of this day, so I am entering into the eternity of that Day.

John Donne, the poet, puts it so much more reverently. In his earlier life as a lecherous dilettante, Donne would often despise the sunrise for the way it intruded on his fleshly desires. Who has not read Donne and smiled at his image of the 'unruly sun' disturbing the two lovers in bed. 'Must to thy motions lovers' seasons run?' he asks of the sun.[23] Later on, however, Donne developed a keen and poetic sense of the eternal blessing contained in a life of daily attentiveness to God in prayer: 'God hath made no decree to distinguish the seasons of his mercies; in paradise, the fruits were ripe, the first minute, and in heaven it is alwaies Autumne, his mercies are ever in their maturity.' Thus, he opines, 'We ask *panem quotidianam*, our daily bread, and God never sayes you should have come yesterday, he never sayes you must againe to morrow, but to day if you will heare his voice, to day he will heare you.'[24] In other words, today contains all there is: not in the sense that the past and the future collapse into some eternal present in which we are trapped – that way lies the cyclical imprisonment of Eastern mysticism – but in the sense that the horizon of our future hope, by the Spirit, rushes into the present of today, filling it with intimations and anticipations of glory.

The Last Days

Viewing time in this way resolves the old mantras that gather around end-time prophecies, and last days apocalyptic. Our Christian sub-culture is full of them at the moment. In certain fundamentalist circles in North America we hear of nothing else except Last Days predictions. However, the Last Days in the New Testament is not so much an end time apocalyptic but a gospel announcement that in the death and resurrection of Jesus Christ, and the coming of the Spirit, the future has broken into the present tense. The end has begun. The future Kingdom of God has been inaugurated. Repeatedly and consistently in the New Testament, we are encouraged to see the Last Days as the intersection of future glory with present reality in Christ, rather than an escape from reality. For certain, our hope has not yet been consummated. The coming of Christ has yet to occur. But neither must we idly wait, for what the church celebrates, from Advent to Pentecost, is nothing less than *the* great End-Time event. Life in the Spirit is not just a whiff of paradise lost, but a first-fruits of the celestial city. It is the Day One of creation, in much the same way as Augustine argued, but in entering *this* day of creation we find we are entering into *that* Day of creation too – the eschaton, to put it more technically. As Luther realised, we have only two days to pay attention to: this day and that Day. And by living this day well, the argument in this book leads us to suppose that we are living in the eternity of that Day – one that has been anticipated from the very beginning.

My hope, in putting things in these terms, is to make eternity far more believable. Like most Christians, I too have difficulties imagining what glory will be like. Furthermore, the way the second coming of Christ is portrayed in the popular Christian media can sometimes leave one cold. It is as if Christ is intruding into a world hitherto ignorant of his presence; as if the only way we can possibly imagine him is as 'a thief in the night'. It is a biblical image, to be sure, and one that pertains, Paul says, to those who belong to the night, asleep in their dissipation.[25] But 'we do not belong to the night or to the darkness'. Rather, 'You are all sons of the light and sons of the day.' Paul is not simply lending his weight to that suspicion of night-time activities so deeply entrenched in the religious imagination, but underlining that the reason Christian existence in the present time is like unto a day is because it ushers forth from that Day – the day of the Lord. In that sense the Parousia – the coming of the Lord – is not simply an event in the future, but something that is present to us every day of our lives. The reason it will not be a surprise to us who believe, picking up Paul's argument once again, is because we are already sons of the day.

Theologians will accuse me here of collapsing the future into the present – or, to put it more technically, forsaking the return of Christ in the cause of realised eschatology, or even Christian existentialism – but such is not my intention, nor my conviction. The Parousia remains out there on its own as a distinct article in the creed and a moment in time and history: 'I believe he will come again, to judge the living and the dead,' says the creed. My point, however, is that daily living in Christ, in faith, hope and love, is an anticipation if not a participation in the glory of that Day, the rushing of eternal life into the present moment, to the extent that time, in one sense, ceases to be something quantitative but rather something qualitative. Eternity is not, as P.T. Forsyth argued, 'a second order of things, which might be developed out of time or inserted into it, but which is less obvious, less real, more ghostly and metaphorical'. Rather, 'all the deepest life is timeless; and the more life there is the more timeless it feels. The more intensely we live the less we take note of the passing of time. Life is full of the present the more vital it is.'[26]

This is why – going back to the challenge Os Guinness laid down – we have to deal theologically with the notion of time. Lest our efforts be in vain, 'redeeming the time' as an intentional Christian project must be at the heart of Christian mission. Churches can run their programmes and write their mission statements all they want but if the Christians live their lives just as anxiously and as distractedly as the rest of the world, what difference does it make? Why would anyone want to join our Christian communities, if all they experience is a glorified, slightly baptised form of what they already have in the world? They may as well stay at home.

Furthermore, the project to redeem time ought to be more than just an existential experience; it ought to be practical. The redemption of time must find concrete expression in distinct practices. Sabbath keeping, Lord's Day worship, early morning prayer, praying the psalms, one day at a time contracts, prayer for daily bread, table fellowship, hospitality, practising the presence of God, evening worship – these are not luxuries but necessary adjuncts to a theology of grace. They are not the preferences of an ageing Christian who has discovered the riches of the liturgical tradition late on. They are the essential practices of faith by which grace, of whatever spiritual tradition, finds concrete and habituated response in the people of God. Pietistic faith is all well and good. It is a veritable tradition, and one that many of us have grown up in. But pietistic faith alone will not be adequate for the challenges that will face the church in the years to come. What the church needs now is intense faith: Christianity that finds concrete expression in a rule of faith.

It is important to recognise that such a rigorous approach to faith is not any less gospel. Practising solitude, for example – or prayer, or rest, or hospitality – is not Christian faith taking its place alongside the many other competing spiritualities out there, any more than it is the translation of living faith into dull routines. Whilst there are many parallels between what Christians practise and what, say, a Buddhist practises in terms of contemplation, I am anxious to underline that what I offer here is a distinctively, and uniquely, gospel-centred approach. As Bonhoeffer wrote in *The Cost of Discipleship* about the practice of taking a day at a time: '"Be not anxious for the morrow." This is not to be taken as a philosophy of life, or as a moral law: it is the gospel of Jesus Christ and only so can it be understood. Only those who follow him and know him can receive this word as a promise of the love of his Father and the deliverance from the thraldom of material things.'[27]

But precisely because it is a promise of Jesus, it is to be taken seriously by those who follow him. To think one can survive simply on a diet of pietistic enthusiasm without intense discipline is like a budding pianist thinking she can perform in the concert halls of the world without serious practice. Radical discipleship is the flip side of the gospel of grace. The discipline of the secret, as Bonhoeffer goes on to say, is the mainstay of real and genuine faith. And though the threat of legalism is always near to such a way, my sense at the moment is that this will not be our problem. On the contrary, our fear of Pharisaism is precisely what is keeping us from fleshing out a faith that will really cut it with the world. Relevance is everything. The audience is king. Whereas in previous generations Christians might be tutored in the way of discipleship, we have settled for an easy believism, a one-time decisionism. For Christian culture to genuinely survive the next few decades it must go beyond this. It must renounce the desire for quick fixes and the security of numerical success, and instead pursue 'a long obedience in the same direction'.[28] Christian growth is slow work. It is organic rather than mechanic. It requires attentiveness not rush. In order for Christian communities to truly survive the 24/7 world, those who are responsible for the spiritual formation of the church will have to go deeper rather than quicker. If I am in any way correct in my thesis, time in particular will need to go slower, for only then will the church be fully able to appreciate the grace invested in each new day. As Forsyth put it, trying to describe the difference between our time and God's time: 'We ask, how long, instead of how rich, how full we live.'[29]

Thus, without wanting to confuse the reader with yet more time travelling – we are back where we began: namely how to break the incessant busyness and increasing speed of modern living. It is precisely the speed of modern living, we argued earlier, that means we are hardly present for anything. But by living a day well: embracing its uniqueness, entering its slowness, accepting its messiness, we end up celebrating its holiness. Forsyth once again:

> Our eternal life is not at the end of our days but at the heart of them, the source of them, the control of them. Time is there to reveal or deposit Eternity, not to qualify for it. Eternity does not lie at the other end of time, it pervades it. We can invert our way of putting it. Time is, as it were, the precipitate of eternity – should I say the secretion of it? Time is the living garment of the God in us.[30]

I am writing this at seven a.m. on Tuesday 12 June 2007. As has been the case with writing most of this book, I have been up a couple of hours already. The dawn chorus was especially good this morning. One of my sons has just emerged and is busy eating his breakfast. I am tempted to listen to the seven o'clock news. I have a full day ahead of me. I embrace it in prayer for what it is. I do not want to miss any of it, its joys or its sadnesses. I want to be present for all of it. I am tired of rushing my life away, and my children are tired of me doing that too. I am not master of my destiny, nor the captain of my soul. I belong to another. And this is the day that the Lord has made, so I will rejoice and be glad in it, rehearsing the drama of that day, when time as we know it will be no more, and God will be all in all.

Endnotes

Preface

[1] Genesis 1:5.

[2] M. Marshall, *Free to Worship: Creating Transcendent Worship Today* (London: Marshall Pickering, 1996), 143.

1. Gospel Rhythms

[1] C. Aziz, *The Olive Readers* (London: Pan, 2006), 279.

[2] *The Truman Show*, produced by Edward. S. Feldman, et al., directed by Peter Weir, Paramount Pictures, 1998.

[3] W. Brueggemann, *Ichabod Toward Home: The Journey of God's Glory* (Grand Rapids/Cambridge: Eerdmans, 2002), 121–122.

[4] See D.J. Taylor, *On the Corinthian Spirit: The Decline of Amateurism in Sport* (London: Yellow Jersey Press, 2006).

[5] See N. Klein, *No Logo: Taking Aim at the Brand Bullies* (Toronto: Vintage, 2000); also B.J. Walsh and S.C. Keesmaat, *Colossians Remixed: Subverting the Empire* (Downers Grove: IVP, 2004), for an imaginative reworking of the Colossians text, drawing parallels between the imperial claims of Rome and modern globalisation. Their call is for the church to act subversively in the light of the gospel which announces not simply a privatised faith, but the Lordship of Christ over every sphere of life.

[6] See C. Iggulden and H. Iggulden, *The Dangerous Book for Boys* (London: HarperCollins, 2006), for a wonderful reminder of the lost world of knots, treehouses and tales of incredible courage.

[7] See H. Cox, *The Feast of Fools: A Theological Essay on Festivity and Fantasy* (New York/Evanston and London, Harper & Row, 1970), 9.

[8] See J. Barzun, *From Dawn to Decadence: 1500 to the Present, 500 Years of Western Cultural Life* (London: HarperCollins, 2000); and also M. Berman, *The Twilight of American Culture* (New York/London: W.W. Norton, 2001).

[9] See www.waghotels.com

[10] See M. Phillips, *Londonistan: How Britain is Creating a Terror State Within* (London: Gibson Square, 2006).

[11] A. O'Hear, 'Diana, Queen of Hearts' in D. Anderson and P. Mullen (ed.), *Faking It: The Sentimentalisation of Modern Society* (London: Penguin, 1998), 181–190.

[12] A. MacIntyre, *After Virtue: A Study in Moral Theology* (London: Duckworth, 1985), 262–263.

[13] R. Bauckham, 'Time and Eternity' in R. Bauckham (ed.), *God Will Be All in All: the Eschatology of Jürgen Moltmann* (Minneapolis: Fortress), 155–226.

[14] M. Hoog, *Musée de l'Orangerie: The Nymphéas of Claude Monet* (Paris: Réunion des Musées Nationaux, 2006), 107.

[15] S. Cottrell, *Do Nothing to Change Your Life: Discovering What Happens When You Stop* (London: Church House Publishing, 2001), 75.

[16] B.J. Miller-McLemore, 'Contemplation in the Midst of Chaos: Contesting the Maceration of the Theological Teacher' in L. Gregory Jones and S. Paulsell (eds.), *The Scope of our Art: The Vocation of the Theological Teacher* (Grand Rapids/Cambridge: Eerdmans, 2002), 48–74.

[17] Luke 10:38–42.

[18] See R. Banks, *The Tyranny of Time: When 24 hours is not Enough* (Downers Grove: IVP, 1983).

[19] Abbot C. Jamison, *Finding Sanctuary: Monastic Steps for Everyday Life* (London: Weidenfeld & Nicolson, 2006), 36–38.

[20] D. Steindl-Rast and S. Lebell, *Music of Silence: A Sacred Journey through the Hours of the Day* (Berkeley: Seastone, 2002), 3.

[21] O. Guinness, *Prophetic Untimeliness: A Challenge to the Idol of Relevance* (Grand Rapids: Baker Books, 2003), 9–23.

[22] Ecclesiastes 3:1ff.

[23] D. Bonhoeffer, *Life Together* (London: SCM, 1992), 27.

[24] Q.J. Shultze, *Habits of the High-Tech Heart: Living Virtuously in the Information Age* (Grand Rapids: Baker Academic, 2002), 68.

[25] D.C. Bass, *Receiving the Day: Christian Practices for Opening the Gift of Time* (San Francisco: Jossey-Bass, 2001), 121–122. I came across this book a month before sending my own manuscript to the editors.

Engaging with her book – nervously of course, since we reflect on the same theme – and looking through her bibliography in particular, I can see that we found inspiration in many of the same places.

[26] For a reading of the gospel through these different concepts of time see H. Rayment-Pickard, *The Myths of Time: From St Augustine to American Beauty* (London: Darton, Longman & Todd, 2004).

[27] N. Maclean, *A River Runs Through It, and Other Stories* (Chicago and London: University of Chicago Press, 1976), 44.

[28] Ibid., 2.

2. One Day at a Time, Sweeet Jesus

[1] Luke 9:23.

[2] Matthew 6:34.

[3] Matthew 6:27; 'Who of you by worrying can add a single hour to his life?'

[4] It is worth quoting Edward Bounds in full: 'To-day's manna is what we need; tomorrow God will see that our needs are supplied. This is the faith which God seeks to inspire. So leave tomorrow with its cares, its needs, its troubles, in God's hands. There is no storing tomorrow's grace or tomorrow's praying; neither is there any laying-up of today's grace, to meet tomorrow's necessities. We cannot have tomorrow's grace, we cannot eat tomorrow's bread, we cannot do tomorrow's praying. "Sufficient unto the day is the evil thereof;" and most assuredly, if we possess faith, sufficient also, will be the good.' E.M. Bounds, *The Necessity of Prayer* (Fearn: Christian Publications, 2006), 20–21.

[5] Matthew 10:19.

[6] See http://homepage.ntlworld.com/gary.hart/lyricism/martell.html.

[7] Psalm 90:12.

[8] A. Dillard, *Pilgrim at Tinker Creek* (London: Pan, 1976), 20.

[9] See C. Honoré, *In Praise of Slow: How a Worldwide Movement is Challenging the Cult of Speed* (London: Orion, 2005). For those of us seeking to explore alternative ways of being church, the Slow movement, originating in the slow food movement in Italy, is very intriguing. There is now a protest in the culture at large, it seems, against the increasing rapidity of modern living. Whether slow food will translate into slow driving, however, is a moot point, for, as Honoré points out, it is unlikely you will ever get an Italian to drive slowly.

[10] James 4:15.

[11] I would like to pay tribute here to the nearby Loseley House Cancer Support Group. Since arriving in Guildford, it has been my privilege to attend their meetings as a guest speaker, and I always go away from those times having received far more than I give. The practice of living one day at a time with faith and gratitude is particularly strong among these wonderful people. See J. More-Molyneux, *The Loseley Challenge* (London: Hodder and Stoughton, 1995), 187–199.

[12] See K. Bailey, *Poet and Peasant and Through Peasant Eyes: A Literary-Cultural Approach to the Parables in Luke's Gospel* (Grand Rapids: Eerdmans, 1976), 55–73.

[13] K. Norris, 'The Aridity of Grace and Other Comedies' from *Portland* magazine, quoted in M. Silf, *The Way of Wisdom* (Oxford: Lion Hudson, 2006), 90.

[14] G. Bernanos, *The Diary of a Country Priest*, trans. Pamela Morris (London: Fount, 1977), 234.

[15] See R. Inchausti, *Subversive Orthodoxy: Outlaws, Revolutionaries, and Other Christians in Disguise* (Grand Rapids: Brazos, 2005).

[16] P. Shaffer, *Equus* (London: Penguin, 1974), 82–83.

[17] See F. Beuchner, *The Alphabet of Grace* (San Franciso: Harper, 1989).

[18] See K. Norris, *The Cloister Walk* (New York: Riverhead, 1996).

[19] W. Berry, *Fidelity: Five Stories* (New York and San Francisco: Pantheon, 1992), 20.

[20] I attribute this wisdom to Lewis Smedes, who I once heard deliver the most heart-warming sermons about marriage. Christian marriage is indeed a challenge and for the married it is central to Christian discipleship. After all, as Smedes rightly discerns, everyone marries a fantasy. Christian discipleship is about discarding the fantasy and embracing the infinite mystery of the reality. For the best book on the nature of marriage see M. Mason, *The Mystery of Marriage* (London: Triangle, 1997).

[21] R. Williams, *Silence and Honey Cakes: The Wisdom of the Desert* (Oxford: Lion/Medio Media, 2003), 97.

[22] Mark 8:34.

[23] Luke 9:23.

[24] For a view of Luke's theology as a weakening of the primitive eschatology of the early Christians see H. Conzelmann, *The Theology of St Luke*, London: SCM, 1960, 95–136.

[25] Luke 9:24.

3. Sabbath Rest

[1] Psalm 92.

[2] D.C. Bass, 'Keeping Sabbath' in D.C. Bass (ed.), *Practicing our Faith: A Way of Life for Searching People* (San Francisco: Jossey-Bass, 1997), 72.

[3] *Chariots of Fire*, produced by David Puttnam, directed by Hugh Hudson, Warner Brothers, 1981.

[4] M.J. Dawn, *Keeping the Sabbath Wholly: Ceasing, Resting, Embracing, Feasting* (Grand Rapids: Eerdmans, 1989), xiii.

[5] Mark 2:27.

[6] See Matthew 12:9–14; Luke 13:10–17; Luke 14:1–16; John 5:1–17, 9:1–41.

[7] Mark 2:28.

[8] E.H. Peterson, *Working the Angles: The Shape of Pastoral Integrity* (Eerdmans: Grand Rapids, 1987), 46.

[9] Sabbath comes from the Hebrew *shabbat*, which crudely put means 'to cease'. Lest we get too esoterical in our theology, let us remember that sabbath simply means 'stop'.

[10] W. Brueggemann, *Genesis, Interpretation: a Bible Commentary for Teaching and Preaching* (Atlanta: John Knox Press, 1982), 35.

[11] M. Luther, 'Treatise on Good Works' in *The Christian in Society* I, trans. W.A. Lambert, Revd James Atkinson, vol. 44 of *Luther's Works*, general editor, Helmut. T. Lehmann (Philidelphia: Fortress, 1966), 72.

[12] A.J. Heschel, *The Sabbath: Its Meaning for Modern Man* (Boston: Shambhala Publications, 2003 [1951]), 13.

[13] The fact that Job cursed the seventh day (for he had sat with his friends for seven days) declaring I have no rest, is of course the ultimate de-creation story. His world has turned upside down. Nevertheless its very appearance in the structure of the Job narrative pays tribute to its importance within a fully integrated biblical spirituality. See J.G. Janzen, *Job, Interpretation* (Louisville: John Knox, 1985), 66–71.

[14] Genesis 2:2–3.

[15] Hebrews 4:9. 'The weekly Sabbath points to the eternal Sabbath rest and keeps alive the notion that human beings, and thus the whole creation, are on the way to perfection. The world is governed by the messianic time: orientated on being with God in complete freedom and delight.' J. Suurmond, *Word and Spirit at Play: Towards a Charismatic Theology* (London: SCM, 1994), 32.

[16] Augustine, *The Confessions*, trans. and ed. P. Burton (London: Everyman's Library, 2001), I.I.I.

17 Suurmond, *Word and Spirit*, 32–37.
18 Heschel, *The Sabbath*, xvii.
19 M. Buchanan, *The Holy Wild: Trusting in the Character of God* (Sisters: Multnomah, 2003), 212.
20 Deuteronomy 5:15.
21 Bass, 'Keeping Sabbath', 81.
22 See N.T. Wright, *What Saint Paul Really Said* (Grand Rapids: Eerdmans, 1997), for an introduction to what is termed by New Testament scholars 'Fresh Perspectives' on Paul.
23 Quoted in Dawn, *Keeping the Sabbath Wholly*, 42.
24 See D. Willard, *The Great Omission* (San Francisco: HarperCollins, 2006).
25 G. Dix, *The Shape of the Liturgy* (London; A & C Black, 1986, 2nd ed.), 336–337.
26 Exodus 23:10–11; Leviticus 25:8–55; Luke 4:18–19.
27 For this reason we ought to ban church business when we gather together on a Sunday. Tempting though it is for committees to meet on a Sunday, since everyone is already there, there is nothing more inimical to rest, if that is indeed what we want our Sundays to be, than worship followed by business.
28 Heschel, *The Sabbath*, 1.
29 Ibid., 19.
30 Ibid., 12.
31 Ibid., 12.
32 W. Berry, *Sabbaths* (San Francisco: North Point Press, 1987), 19.

Interlude: A Sermon on Naboth's Vineyard

1 See the introduction by C. Schwobel in C.E. Gunton, *Theology for Preaching: Sermons for Brentwood* (Edinburgh: T&T Clark, 2001), 1–20.
2 W. Brueggemann, *Smyth & Helwys Bible Commentary: 1 & 2 Kings* (Macon: Smyth & Helwys, 2000), 265.
3 I.W. Provan, *1 and 2 Kings*, *New International Biblical Commentary* (Peabody: Hendrickson/Carlisle: Paternoster, 1995), 157.

Prologue to Part Two

1 Psalm 55:16-17.

4. Your Mercies are New Every Morning

[1] G.M. Hopkins, *God's Grandeur, The Poetry and Prose of Gerard Manley Hopkins* (London: Penguin, 1985), 27.

[2] Psalm 127:2.

[3] Proverbs 27:14.

[4] Psalm 118:24.

[5] Mark 1:35.

[6] Psalm 92:1.

[7] Psalm 143:8.

[8] Psalm 30:5.

[9] Some activities require an early start. 'In Hebrew,' notes Deryck Sheriffs, 'there is a verb for getting up early, the verb sakam.' D. Sheriffs, *The Friendship of the Lord: An Old Testament Spirituality* (Carlisle: Paternoster, 1996), 296.

[10] Bonhoeffer, *Life Together*, 27.

[11] Ibid., 27.

[12] John 20:1. For a fuller discussion of this see N.T. Wright, *Christian Origins and the Question of God, Volume Three: The Resurrection of the Son of God* (London: SPCK, 2003), 667–670.

[13] *Lancelot Andrewes and his Private Devotions* (London: Oliphant, Anderson and Ferrier, 1896), 129.

[14] Ibid., 38.

[15] Ibid., 66.

[16] A. Roger Ekirch, *At Day's Close: A History of Night-time* (London, Phoenix, 2006), 15.

[17] Ibid., 7–30.

[18] Bonhoeffer, *Life Together*, 29.

[19] Ibid., 30.

[20] Ibid., 29.

[21] E.H. Peterson, *Five Smooth Stones for Pastoral Work* (Grand Rapids: Eerdmans/Leominster: Gracewing, 1992), 148.

[22] Bonhoeffer, *Life Together*, 27.

[23] Quoted in P. Yancey, *Prayer? Does it Make a Difference* (London: Hodder, 2006), 115.

[24] J. Moltmann, *In the End – the Beginning* (London: SCM, 2003), 84.

[25] E.H. Peterson, *The Wisdom of Each Other: A Conversation Between Spiritual Friends* (Grand Rapids: Zondervan, 1998), 78–79.

[26] E.H. Peterson, *Working the Angles*, 47–49.

27 Brueggemann, *Genesis*, 30: 'As liturgy, the poetry invites the congregation to confess and celebrate the world as God intended it. Thus, the rhetoric and rhythm of command/execution/assessment permit appropriate antiphons and responses. Giving voice to the poem is itself a line of defense against the press of chaos. It is a way of experiencing the good order of life in the face of the disorder.'

28 S.S. Wesley, arranged by C.F. Manney (Unknown Binding), B.F. Wood Music, 1931.

29 E.H. Peterson, *Working the Angles*, 48.

30 See D. Hansen, *Long Wandering Prayer* (Oxford: The Bible Reading Fellowship, 2001).

31 2 Timothy 1:3; Acts 2:37.

32 M. Robinson, *Gilead* (London: Virago, 2005), 81.

33 Genesis 15:12ff.

34 Exodus 12:29ff.

35 1 Samuel 5:4.

36 Matthew 1:24.

37 Psalm 143:8.

38 T. Merton, *Faith and Violence* (Notre Dame: Notre Dame University Press, 1968), 151.

39 Psalm 2:7.

40 T.S. Eliot, 'Ash Wednesday' in *Collected Poems 1909–1962* (London: Faber & Faber Ltd, 1963), 102.

41 I owe this insight to Terry Virgo, Church of Christ the King, Brighton.

5. Practising the Present

1 G. Herbert, *The Elixir, Poems selected by Jo Shapcott* (London: Faber and Faber, 2006), 95.

2 Psalm 104:22–23.

3 'Great is Thy Faithfulness' by T.O. Chisholm, *Hymns and Psalms* (London: Methodist Publishing House, 1986), Hymn 66.

4 R. Blythe, *Word from Wormingford: A Parish Year* (London: Penguin, 1998).

5 Colossians 3:23.

6 Ecclesiastes 2:24. See also 5:18–20, 8:15.

7 I. Stackhouse, 'Life Between Ministries: A Quiet Word on Tent-Making' in *Ministry Today*: Issue 30, 23–25.

[8] M. Greene, *Thank God it's Monday: Ministry in the Workplace* (London: Scripture Union, 1994).

[9] See P. Stevens, *The Abolition of the Laity: Vocation, Work and Ministry in a Biblical Perspective* (Carlisle: Paternoster, 1999).

[10] See L. Ryken, *Work and Leisure in Christian Perspective* (Leicester: IVP, 1989), for a fuller treatment of this aspect of Reformation theology.

[11] 2 Samuel 16:19.

[12] 2 Samuel 24ff; 2 Samuel 26ff.

[13] Psalm 131:1–2.

[14] 1 Samuel 17:34–37.

[15] E. Crossman, *Mountain Rain: A New Biography of James O Fraser* (Sevenoaks: OMF Books, 1982), 13.

[16] Ibid., 14.

[17] Greene, *Thank God it's Monday*, 21.

[18] A. Kuyper, 'Sphere Sovereignty' in *Abraham Kuyper: A Centennial Reader*, J.D. Bratt (ed.) (Grand Rapids: Eerdmans, 1998), 488.

[19] Evagrius Ponticus, quoted in K. Bazyn: *The Seven Perennial Sins and their Offspring* (New York/London: Continuum, 2004), 158.

[20] Steindl and Lebell, *Music of Silence*, 70–78.

[21] Crossman, *Mountain Rain*, 14.

[22] G. Herbert, *The Elixir*.

[23] P. Hobbs, *The Short Day Dying* (London: Faber and Faber, 2005), 50.

[24] Matthew 6:6.

[25] See Brother Lawrence, *The Practice of the Presence of God*, trans. E.M. Blaiklock (London: Hodder and Stoughton, 1996), 84.

[26] Ibid., 44.

[27] Proverbs 31:15. Incidentally, Bruce Waltke notes in his commentary on this verse the metaphorical meaning of this verse. Like a lioness who hunts for food at night, so this woman 'puts the well being of the household before her own comfort'. See B.K. Waltke, The Book of Proverbs: Chapters 15-31, *The New International Commentary on the Old Testament* (Grand Rapids/Cambridge: Eerdmans, 2005), 524.

[28] 1 John 3:17.

[29] See Bailey, *Poet & Peasant*, 49–50.

[30] See A. Stibbe, *Barefoot in the Kitchen: Bible Readings and Meditations for Mothers* (Oxford: The Bible Reading Fellowship, 2004), 35–40. I am told by one of our young mums that this book proved a huge comfort to her during her own struggles with young children and loss of vocation.

6. Abide with Me, Fast Falls the Eventide

[1] Compline, *Common Worship: Sermons and Prayers for the Church of England* (Church House Publishing, 2008), 81–89.

[2] Compline derives from the word *completorium*, meaning completion.

[3] Quoted in D. Scott, *Sacred Tongues: The Golden Age of Spiritual Writing* (London: SPCK, 2001), 19.

[4] J. Baillie, *Christian Devotion* (Oxford: OUP, 1962), 70.

[5] See Matthew 8:23–27, in which Matthew interprets the stilling of the storm episode as an object lesson in faith, or rather lack of faith.

[6] Psalm 127:1–2.

[7] Psalm 121:4.

[8] R. Farrar Capon, *Genesis: The Movie* (Grand Rapids/Cambridge: Eerdmans, 2003), 122.

[9] W. H. Auden, *Selected Poems*, E. Mendelson (ed.) (London: Faber and Faber, 1976), 230.

[10] Psalm 74:16.

[11] S. Chan, *Liturgical Theology: The Church as Worshipping Community* (Downers Grove: IVP Academic, 2006), 163–164.

[12] Psalm 90:14.

[13] A. Dillard, *Holy the Firm* (New York, Hagerstown, San Francisco, London: Harper & Row, 1977), 11.

[14] Andrewes, *Private Devotions*, 146.

[15] Andrewes, *Private Devotions*, 143.

[16] Ibid.

[17] Ephesians 4:26.

[18] Cf. Deuteronomy 24:15: 'Pay him his wages each day before sunset, because he is poor and is counting on it.'

[19] Quoted in A. Lincoln, *Word Biblical Commentary: Ephesians* (Dallas: Word, 1990), 302.

[20] Ibid.

[21] Bonhoeffer, *Life Together*, 55–56.

[22] Quoted in K. Bazyn, *The Seven Perennial Sins and their Offspring* (New York/London: Continuum, 2004), 87.

[23] Psalm 63:6.

[24] Baillie, *Christian Devotion*, 67.

[25] E.H. Peterson, *Working the Angles*, 48.

[26] This idea stems from Capon in *The Foolishness of Preaching* (Grand Rapids: Eerdmans, 1998), 28. As a maxim it is typical of Capon's

whole theological enterprise, which is basically a celebration of death and resurrection. But the point is: it works. As one who is aware of how unbearable he is in the service prior to a sermon, the practice of 'going dead' after finishing the sermon preparation, of letting go and trusting that God will resurrect the sermon when we get there is one I can recommend.

27 Capon, *Genesis*, 32–33.

Interlude: Praying the Psalms

1 Psalm 1.
2 Psalm 55:17.
3 See R. Foster, *Prayer* (London: Hodder and Stoughton, 1992).
4 For a good introduction to Benedictine spirituality see E. de Waal, *Seeking God: The Way of St Benedict* (Norwich: Canterbury Press, 1999).
5 Psalm 1.
6 Psalm 73.
7 Psalm 150. For an introduction and way into praying the Psalms see E.H. Peterson, *Answering God: The Psalms as Tools for Prayer* (San Francisco: Harper & Row, 1989), and W. Brueggemann, *The Message of the Psalms* (Minneapolis: Augsburg, 1984). With typical originality and audacity Brueggemann classifies the Psalms along the lines of Psalms of Orientation, Psalms of Disorientation, Psalms of Reorientation. The Psalms account for both the wintry and the sunny seasons of our life.
8 J. Calvin, *Commentary on the Book of Psalms* (Grand Rapids; Eerdmans, 1949), 1, xxxvii.
9 E.H. Peterson, *Answering God*, 91.
10 Norris, *The Cloister Walk*, 92.
11 Ibid., 91.
12 M. Gilbert, *Sharasnsky: Hero of our Time* (London: Penguin, 1987), 348–351
13 Psalm 22:1.
14 Herbert, 'Prayer' (I), *Selected Poems*, 15.
15 Gilbert, *Sharansky*, 333.
16 Psalm 42: 5.
17 Quoted in *The Psalms with commentary by Kathleen Norris* (New York: Riverhead Books, 1997), ix.

[18] Colossians 3:16.

[19] *The Elephant Man*, produced by Jonathan Sanger, directed by David Lynch, Warner Brothers, 1980.

[20] Psalm 23.

7. Give Us Today Our Daily Bread

[1] A. Simms, *Tescopoly: How One Shop Came Out on Top and Why it Matters* (London: Constable, 2007), 17.

[2] G. Tindall, *Celestine: Voices from a French Village* (London: Minerva, 1996), 88.

[3] Exodus 16:18. For a helpful introduction to the wilderness motif in the Lord's prayer see N.T. Wright, 'The Lord's Prayer as a Paradigm of Christian Prayer' in R. Longenecker (ed.), *Into God's Presence: Prayer in the New Testament* (Grand Rapids/Cambridge: Eerdmans, 2001), 132–154.

[4] Exodus 16:20.

[5] Exodus 16: 22–23.

[6] Exodus 16:12.

[7] Proverbs 30:8–9.

[8] Matthew 6:24.

[9] O. James, *Affluenza* (London: Vermilion, 2007).

[10] Hosea 2:14

[11] Revelation 3:17.

[12] For a devastating critique on how consumerism has affected even our religious behaviour see V.J. Miller, *Consuming Religion: Christian Faith and Practice in a Consumer Culture* (New York/London: Continuum, 2005).

[13] Matthew 4:4.

[14] 1 Corinthians 8:13.

[15] 1 Corinthians 8:15.

[16] See J.H. Yoder, *The Politics of Jesus* (Grand Rapids: Eerdmans, 1972), 66–67. The redress to this situation needs to happen, moreover, not simply at the microlevel of charity, which is where a lot of us Christians get involved, but perhaps more crucially at the macro level where Christian business people are encouraged to invest their time and their money in developing sustainable projects in the developing world. If the biblical concept of Jubilee means anything to

contemporary Christians, whereby debts were released and land was returned every fifty years, then it must replay itself in terms of actual projects in the developing world, as well as at home.

[17] Ezekiel 16:49.

[18] Quoted in T. Chester, *Good News to the Poor: Sharing the Gospel through Social Involvement* (London: IVP, 2004), 103.

[19] W.H. Willimon and S. Hauerwas, *Lord, Teach Us: The Lord's Prayer and Christian Life* (Nashville: Abingdon, 1996), 75.

[20] See S. Van Eman, *On Earth as it is in Advertising: Moving from Commercial Hype to Gospel Hope* (Grand Rapids: Brazos, 2005), for a critical look at how the world of advertising sets up what Van Eman calls a SimGospel: the advertising narrative that simulates the biblical narrative by the seductive promise of happiness through consumption.

[21] See N. Postman, *Amusing Ourselves to Death: Public Discourse in the Age of Show Business* (London: Methuen, 1987), 146–159.

[22] Quoted in E.H. Peterson, *Living the Resurrection: The Risen Christ in Everyday Life* (Colorado Springs: NavPress, 2006), 78.

[23] R. Farrar Capon, *Bed and Board: Plain Talk about Marriage* (New York: Pocket Books 1970), 55.

[24] 1 Timothy 4:3.

[25] Acts 27:35.

[26] Luke 24:13–32.

[27] John 21:1–14.

[28] See P. Berger, *Rumours of Angels* (London: Penguin, 1973), 33–42.

[29] E.H. Peterson, *Living the Resurrection*, 59.

[30] J. Moran, *Queuing for Beginners: The Story of Daily Life from Breakfast to Bedtime* (London: Profile Books, 2007), 20–21.

[31] Galatians 3:28.

[32] Matthew 6:11. See R.T. France, *Matthew: Tyndale New Testament Commentaries* (Grand Rapids/Leicester: Eerdmans/IVP, 1985), 135

[33] R. Lohmeyer, *The Lord's Prayer*, trans. J. Bowden (London: Collins, 1965), 150.

8. The Lord's Day

[1] Revelation 1:10.

[2] A. Collins, *Where Did It All Go Right? Growing Up Normal in the 70s* (London: Ebury Press, 2003), 117.

[3] Justin Martyr, *Apology*, 1.67.

[4] Acts 20:7; 1 Corinthians 16:1; Revelation 1:10.

[5] R.T. Beckwith and W. Stott, *This is the Day: The Biblical Doctrine of the Christian Sunday* (London: Marshall, Morgan & Scott), 1978.

[6] *Didache* 14.

[7] G.W. Lathrop, *Holy Things: A Liturgical Theology* (Minneapolis: Fortress, 1993), 39.

[8] See B.D. Stuhlman, *Redeeming the Time: An Historical and Theological Study of the Church's Rule of Prayer and the Regular Services of the Church* (New York: The Church Hymnal Incorporation, 1992), 69–73.

[9] Lathrop, *Holy Things*, 40.

[10] See C.M. Gay, *The Way of the (modern) World. Or, Why It's Tempting to Live as if God Doesn't Exist* (Grand Rapids/Vancouver/Carlisle: Eerdmans/Regent College/Paternoster, 1998), 31–32. 'It is probably also true that the plausibility of the modern secular outlook is only strengthened by the obsessive attention the modern mass media give to political theatre, for such attention simply reinforces the impression that there is nothing else in the world that really matters, indeed that all other concerns are either illusory or eventually reducible to the political will power.'

[11] R. Clapp, *A Peculiar People: The Church as Culture in a Post-Christian Society* (Downers Grove: InterVarsity Press, 1996), 195.

[12] See M. Connell, *Eternity Today: On The Liturgical Year*, Volume 2 (New York/London: Continuum, 2006), 1–51, for a sustained treatment of the importance of Sunday within the liturgical cycle.

[13] Luke 24:1.

[14] Luke 24:31; cf. Genesis 3:7.

[15] Acts 2:42.

[16] A. Heschel, *I Asked for Wonder*, Samuel H. Dresner (ed.) (New York, Crossroad, 1983), 20.

[17] M. Buber, *I and Thou*, trans. R.G. Smith (Edinburgh: T&T Clark, 1999 [1937]).

[18] E.H. Peterson, *Reversed Thunder: The Revelation of John and the Praying Imagination* (San Francisco: HarperCollins, 1991), 70.

[19] See M. Buchanan, *Your God is Too Safe: Rediscovering the Wonder of a God You Can't Control* (Sisters: Multnomah, 2001), 218–235.

[20] E. Underhill, *Collected Papers* (London: Longmans, Green and Co., 1946), 78; quoted in E.H. Peterson, *Reversed Thunder*, 71.

[21] Hebrews 12:22–24.

[22] I. Stackhouse, *The Problem of Immediacy in Charismatic Worship*, MTh Thesis, London Bible College, 1997.

[23] Clapp, *A Peculiar People*, 112.

[24] Ibid., 116.

[25] Not only does the church need a charismatic renewal; it needs also a liturgical renewal. These two impulses are not irreconcilable; they are necessary partners. I develop this idea further, with special reference to the sacraments, in I. Stackhouse, 'God's Transforming Presence: Spirit Empowered Worship and its Mediation' in A. Walker and L. Bretherton (eds.) *Remembering Our Future: Explorations in Deep Church* (Carlisle: Paternoster, 2007), 150–169.

[26] Lathrop, *Holy Things*, 39.

9. Time, Space, Rhythm, and Place

[1] W. Blake, 'Auguries of Innocence' in *A Choice of Blake's Verse*, selected with an Introduction by Kathleen Raine (London: Faber and Faber, 1970), 31.

[2] J. O'Connor, *Redemption Falls* (London: Harvill Secker, 2007), 5.

[3] M. Boroson, *The One Moment Master: Stillness for People on the Go* (London: Rider, 2007), 67.

[4] 2 Peter 3:8.

[5] Psalm 84:10.

[6] J.-Pierre de Caussade, *The Sacrament of the Present Moment*, trans. Kitty Muggeridge from the original text of *Self-Abandonment to Divine Providence* (San Francisco: Harper, 1989). As Richard Foster points out in the Introduction to this latest edition: 'The spirituality of de Caussade is so utterly practical and down to earth. He takes the moments of our days and the simple duties that make up those moments and gives them sacramental significance.' xviii.

[7] J. Moltmann, *In the End – the Beginning*, trans. Margaret Koll (London: SCM, 2004) 17.

[8] D. Paterson, *The Book of Shadows* (London: Picador, 2004), 25.

[9] 1 Timothy 6:12.

[10] 1 Corinthians 10:11.

[11] 1 Timothy 6:19.

[12] See R. Bauckham (ed.), *God Will Be All in All: The Eschatology of Jürgen Moltmann* (Minneapolis: Fortress, 2001), 155–226, for a fuller discussion

of this contrast, with reference to the eschatological aesthetics of Moltmann. Bauckham goes on to explore the concept of eternal time as opposed to linear, historical time in the novel *To the Lighthouse*, by Virginia Woolf, and also in the series of paintings by Monet, the *Nymphéas*, refered to above, and housed in the Orangerie in Paris. In both works of art, Bauckham claims, the artist is seeking to preserve the transient, attributing it with eternal value.

[13] Quoted in M. Mayne, *The Enduring Melody* (London: Darton, Longman and Todd, 2006), 197.

[14] S. Kierkegaard, *Fear and Trembling and The Book on Adler*, trans. W. Lowrie, Everyman's Library (London: Alfred A. Knopf, 1994, [1941]), 30–31.

[15] C. Moore (ed.), *Provocations: The Spiritual Writings of Kierkegaard* (Farmington: Plough Publishing House, 1999), 211–212.

[16] Moltmann, *In the End*, 153.

[17] Ibid., 159–160.

[18] Lamentations 3:22.

[19] Augustine, *The Confessions*, 11:14:16, 270.

[20] *Groundhog Day*, produced by Trevor Albert and Harold Ramis, directed by Harold Ramis, Colombia Pictures 1993.

[21] E. Farajeon, 'Morning Has Broken' in *Songs of Fellowship 1*, Hymn 393 (Eastbourne: Kingsway, 1999).

[22] Hebrews 3:7–11.

[23] In the most recent John Donne biography John Stubbs notes that Donne's father-in-law Sir George More was something of an amateur scholar. His treatise *A Demonstration of God in His Workes* was something of a tract on the existence of God, and it may well be, Stubbs notes, that Donne's poem 'The Sunne Rising' was something of a riposte to More. See J. Stubbs, *Donne: The Reformed Soul* (London: Penguin, 2007), 178.

[24] J. Donne, *No Man Is an Island: A Selection from the Prose of John Donne*, selected and edited by Rivers Scott (London: The Folio Society, 1997), 143.

[25] 1 Thessalonians 5:1–8.

[26] P.T. Forsyth, *This Life and the Next: The Effect on this Life of Faith in Another* (London: Macmillan and Co., 1918), 70–71.

[27] D. Bonhoeffer, *The Cost of Discipleship* (London: SCM, 1964 [1937]), 159.

[28] The phrase is Nietzsche's and used with surprising effect as the title of Peterson's pioneering book on Christian spirituality. See E.H.

Peterson, *A Long Obedience in the Same Direction: Discipleship in an Instant Society*, 20th anniversary edition (Downers Grove: IVP, 2000).

[29] Forsyth, *This Life and the Next*, 67–68.

[30] Ibid., 73.

Index

activism 10, 39
apocalyptic 27, 116, 120, 133
Acts 151
Andrewes, L. 55–56, 83–84
Auden, W.H. 80–81
Augustine 33, 126, 132, 134
Aziz, C. 138

Bailey, K.E. 141
Baillie, J. 79, 86
Bakke, R. 106
Banks, R. 139
Barzun, J. 139
Bass, D.C. 14, 29, 35
Bauckham, R. 119
Bazyn, K. 146, 147
Beckwith, R.T. 115
Benedict 8
Benedictine 25, 72, 91, 93
Berger, P. 150
Berman, M. 139
Bernanos, G. 22
Berry, W. 26, 41
Beuchner, F. 141
Blake, W. 152
Blythe, R. 65
Bonhoeffer, D. 13, 55–58, 85, 136
Borgmann, A. 108

Boroson, M. 127
Bounds, E.M. 140
Brother L. 74
Browne, T. 85
Brueggemann, W. 4, 32, 43–44
Buber, M. 151
Buchanan, M. 34
busyness 5, 38, 59, 110, 137

Calvin, J. 4, 67, 92
Capon, R.F. 80, 88–89, 108, 147–148
Caussade, J-P. de 152
Chan, S. 81
Chariots of Fire 30
Chester, T. 150
Christendom 7, 38, 115
chronos 11–12, 60, 128–129
Clapp, R. 117, 123
Collins, A. 113
Colossians 138, 145
commodity 44, 46–47
compline 77, 80–81, 84, 88, 147
Connell, M. 151
consumer/ism 9, 33, 104, 107–108, 122
contemplative 10–11, 60, 128–129
Conzelmann, H. 141
Corinthians (1) 149, 152
Cottrell, S. 139

Cox, H. 7
Crossman, E. 69

David 68–69, 95
Dawn, M.J. 30
Deuteronomy 35, 46, 105, 143, 147
Didache 116
Dillard, A. 21, 82
discipline 13, 18–19, 37–39, 55, 58, 86, 136
discipleship 16–17, 27, 70, 85, 91, 103–104, 136, 141, 153–154
Dix, G. 143
dominicum 115–116
Donne, J. 133

Ecclesiastes 12, 65, 139
Ecclesiasticus 57
Egypt 35, 46, 102–103
Ekirch, A.R., 56–57
Elephant Man (The) 96
Eliot, T.S. 63
Ephesians 85
Equus (Peter Shaffer) 23–24
eschatology/eschatological 13–14, 39, 111, 116, 126, 134, 141, 153
existential/ism 3, 17, 80, 126, 130, 135
Evagrius Ponticus 146
Ezekiel 106
Exodus 35, 143, 145, 149

Forsyth, P.T. 135–137
France, R.T. 150

Gay, C.M. 151
Genesis 13, 32–33, 56, 87, 108, 132, 138, 142, 145, 151
Gilbert, M. 148
gnostic/gnosticism 26, 65, 121–122

Greene, M. 67, 71
Groundhog Day 132
Guinness, O. 12, 135
Gunton, C.E. 143

Hansen, D. 145
Hamm, A. 37–38
Hartley, D. 47
Hebrews 132, 142, 151
Herbert, G. 72–73, 148
Heschel, A. 33–34, 40, 93, 119
Hobbs, P. 73
Honoré, C. 140
Hoog, M. 139
Hopkins, G.M. 53, 128, 144
Hosea 149

Ignatius 88–89
Iggulden, C.H. 138
Inchausti, R. 23

James 22
James, O. 149
Jamison, A.C. 139
Janzen, J.G. 142
John 55, 75, 142, 146, 150
John (Revelation) 120

kairos 11–12, 14, 128
Kierkegaard, S. 126, 129–130
Kuyper, A. 71
Kings (1 and 2) 44
Klein, N. 138

Lamentations 57–58
Laodicea 104
Lathrop, G.W. 116, 124–125
Lebell, S. 139
leisure 3–6, 21, 107–108

Leviticus 143
Lewis, C.S. 96
Lohmeyer, R. 150
Lord's Day 8, 13, 30, 38, 55, 113–125, 127, 129, 131, 133, 135–137
Loseley House 141
Luke 27, 111, 118, 139, 140, 141, 142, 143, 150–151
Luther, M. 32, 67, 134
Lutheran 58

MacIntyre, A. 8
Maclean, N. 14–15
Mark 27, 142, 144
Marshall, M. ix
Martell, L. 18
Martyr, J. 115
Mason, M. 141
Matthew 62, 111, 140, 142, 146, 147, 149
Merton, T. 62–63, 78, 83
Miller-McLemore, B.J. 10
Miller, V.J. 149
Moltmann, J. 59, 131
monastic/monasticism 8–11, 24–26, 51, 80, 85–88
Monet, C. 9, 153
Moore, C. 153
mothers 76, 146
More-Molyneux, J 141
Moran, J. 109
mystic/ism 10, 40, 51, 82, 119, 130, 133

Norris, K. 22, 93, 141, 148

O'Connor, J. 126
O Fraser, J. 69–70, 72
O'Hear, A. 139
Paterson, D. 129

Paul 31, 37, 59, 69, 84, 93, 96, 105, 108, 109, 129, 134
Peter (1) 127
Peterson, E.H. xi, 31, 60–61, 87, 92–93, 109, 120, 153–154
piety/pietistic 8, 74, 106, 135–136
Pharisaical/Pharisaism 53, 136
Phillips, M. 139
Plutarch 84
Postman, N. 150
post-modern/ity 7, 117
Protestant 32–33, 37-38
Provan, I.W. 44
Proverbs 54, 75, 146, 149
Psalms 8, 20, 29, 51–54, 57, 59, 61–62, 65, 68–69, 79, 81–83, 86, 91–97, 128, 132, 135

Rayment-Pickard, H. 140
Revelation 120, 149, 150, 151
Robinson, M. 61–62
Ryken, L. 146
sabbath 4, 6, 8, 13, 29–41, 47, 66, 86–87, 102, 112, 115, 118, 124–5, 134, 142
Samuel (1 and 2) 145, 146
Schwobel, C. 143
Scott, D. 147
Sharansky, A. 94–95
Sheriffs, D. 144
Shultze, Q.J. 14
Silf, M. 141
Simms, A. 149
sleep 13, 19, 41, 56, 59–61, 77–89, 134
Smedes, L. 141
Steindl-Rast, D. 139
Stevens, P. 67
Stibbe, A. 76
Stott, W. 115

Stubbs, J. 153
Stuhlman, B.D. 151
St Gervais ix
Suurmond, J-J. 142–143

Taylor, D.J. 138
Taylor, J. 56
Taylor, J. 26
technology/technological 11, 33, 44, 47
Thessalonians (1) 153
time management 5, 60
Timothy (1) 150, 152
Tindall, G. 149
Truman Show (The) 3
Tutu, D. 59

24/7 6, 15, 87–88, 127, 136

Underhill, E. 120
utility, utilitarian/ism 33, 38

Van Eman, S. 150

Waal, E. de 148
Waltke, B.K. 146
Wesley, S. 61
Wesley, S. 74
Whyte, A. 56
wilderness 102–103, 105, 132, 149
Willard, D. 143
Williams, R. 27
Willimon, W.H 150
Wisdom of Solomon 57
Wright, N.T. 143, 144

Yancey, P. 144
Yoder, J.H. 149

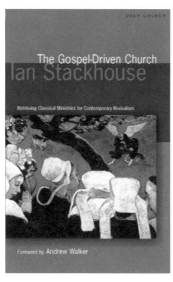

The Gospel-Driven Church

Retrieving Classical Ministries for Contemporary Revivalism

Ian Stackhouse

Charismatic Renewal has at the core of its ideology an aspiration for revival. This is a laudable aspiration, but in recent years, in the absence of large-scale evangelistic impact, such a vision has encouraged a faddist mentality among many Charismatic church leaders.

The Gospel-Driven Church documents this development and the numerous theological and pastoral distortions that take place when genuine revival fervour transmutes into revivalism. Ian Stackhouse shows how a retrieval of some of the core practices of the church – preaching, the sacraments, the laying on of hands and prayer – are essential at this moment in the Charismatic Renewal. He commends a recovery of the classical 'means of grace' as a way of keeping the church centred on the gospel rather than on mere concerns about numbers.

> 'A model of careful biblical and spiritual discernment, both appreciative and cautionary. I find him a most welcome ally in our "stay against confusion".' – **Eugene Peterson**, Professor Emeritus of Spiritual Theology, Regent College, Vancouver BC, Canada

Ian Stackhouse is Pastoral Leader of Guildford Baptist Church, UK.

978-1-84227-290-9

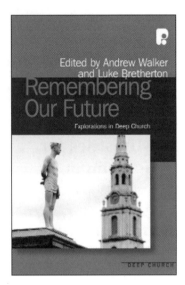

Remembering Our Future

Explorations in Deep Church

Edited by Andrew Walker and Luke Bretherton

Many are exasperated with what they perceive as the fad-driven, one-dimensional spirituality of modern evangelicalism. Instead they desire to reconnect with, and be deeply rooted in, the common historical Christian tradition as well as their evangelical heritage: Welcome to what C.S. Lewis called 'Deep Church'. At its heart Deep Church is about remembering our past in order to face our future. *Remembering Our Future* raises some very compelling questions for both emerging and inherited church leaders as it offers a new vision of living traditions of worship, discipleship and service. One of the most important questions this thoughtful book asks is, 'How can we both listen to the wisdom of ages past and be open to the on-going creative work of God today?'

> 'These essays are the best attempt I have come across to address the emerging church's need for a deep ecclesiology. I not only recommend a rigorous contemplation of this book, but also commend its vision of "Deep Church" as a worthy goal for all streams of church life. – **Andrew Jones**, tallskinnykiwi.com and Missional Cell Developer, Church Mission Society

Andrew Walker is Professor of Theology and Education at King's College London and an ecumenical canon of St Paul's Cathedral. **Luke Bretherton** is Lecturer in Theology and Ministry, Convener of the Faith and Public Policy Forum and DMin Programme Director at King's College London.

978-1-84227-504-7

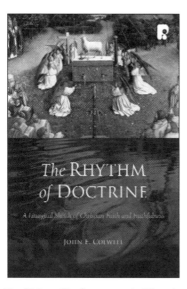

The Rhythm of Doctrine

A Liturgical Sketch of Christian Faith and Faithfulness

John E. Colwell

Traditionally Systematic Theology is structured around the articles of the Creed: the doctrine of God, the doctrine of Christ, the doctrine of the Spirit, the doctrine of the Church, and so on. Whilst this approach has its benefits it is not without flaws. One weakness is that the roots and context of theology in Christian *worship* can be lost sight of and discussions can become abstract and disconnected from the life of faith. But there is another way to structure Systematic Theology, an approach more explicitly and self-consciously rooted in the rhythm of the liturgy followed by most Christians for most of the years of the Church's history.

In *The Rhythm of Doctrine* John Colwell provides a short, inspiring introduction to a Systematic Theology that is built around the worshipful rhythms of the Christian Year. Chapters include the One who comes (Advent); the One who takes our humanity (Christmas); the One who is revealed (Epiphany); the one who journeys to the cross (Lent); the One who lives and reigns (Easter); the One who indwells and transforms (Pentecost); and the One who invites us into communion ('All Saints Day'). In this ancient-future way Christian worship, theology and discipleship are woven into a seamless garment.

John E. Colwell is Tutor in Christian Doctrine and Ethics at Spurgeon's College, London. He is author of *Promise and Presence* and *Living in the Christian Story*.

978-1-84227-498-9

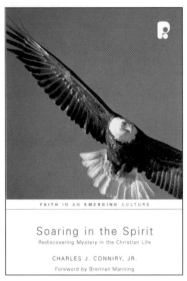

Soaring in the Spirit

Rediscovering Mystery in the Christian Life

Charles J. Conniry, Jr.

This is a book about experiencing the presence of Jesus Christ in the moment-by-moment 'nows' of daily life. James McClendon, Jr. observed that the first task of theology is to locate our place in the story. Like finding directions at a shopping mall with the brightly coloured words, 'you are here,' the author invites us into an encounter with the 'we-are-here' place in God's Great Story. The claim of this book is that the experience of Christ's presence in the 'right-here' of our daily walk – *Christian soaring* – is the birthright of every follower of Jesus Christ. This is a thoughtful, stirring, and ground-breaking book on the neglected topic of *Christian soaring through discerning discipleship.*

'This book is a *tour de force* . . . and can be read with profit by believers and unbelievers, philosophers and theologians, pastors and lay people, and anyone who longs to soar in the Spirit . . . It not only blessed me but drew me to prayer.' – **Brennan Manning**, author of *The Ragamuffin Gospel*.

Charles J. Conniry, Jr. is Associate Professor of Pastoral Ministry and Director of the Doctor of Ministry Program at George Fox Evangelical Seminary, Portland.

978-1-84227-508-5

Chrysalis

The Hidden Transformation in the Journey of Faith

Alan Jamieson

Increasing numbers of Christian people find their faith metamorphosing. Substantial and essential change seems to beckon them beyond the standard images and forms of Christian faith but questions about where this may lead remain. Is this the death of personal faith or the emergence of something new? Could it be a journey that is Spirit-led?

Chrysalis uses the life-cycle of butterflies as a metaphor for the faith journey that many contemporary people are experiencing. Drawing on the three main phases of a butterfly's life and the transformations between these, the book suggests subtle similarities with the zones of Christian faith that many encounter. For butterflies and Christians change between these '*phases*' or '*zones*' is substantial, life-changing and irreversible.

This book accompanies ordinary people in the midst of substantive faith change. It is an excellent resource for those who choose to support others through faith transformations. *Chrysalis* is primarily pastoral and practical drawing on the author's experience of accompanying people in the midst of difficult personal faith changes.

Alan Jamieson is a minister in New Zealand and a trained sociologist. His internationally acclaimed first book, *A Churchless Faith*, researched why people leave their churches to continue their walk of faith outside the church.

978-1-84227-544-3

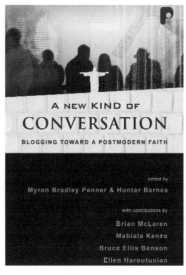

A New Kind of Conversation

Blogging Toward a Postmodern Faith

Edited by Myron Bradley Penner and Hunter Barnes

In the midst of the cultural and intellectual upheavals of post-modernity, evangelicalism finds itself in the middle of a conversation about its own identity and future. The weblog format of this book seeks to give the discussion a postmodern shape that is consistent with its content. This is an experimental book that enters into the conversation through five primary bloggers (Brian McLaren, Bruce Ellis Benson, Ellen Haroutunian, Mabiala Kenzon, and Myron Bradley Penner). Originally posted on anewkindofconversation.com, people all over the world were invited to blog on the following topics:
- What is 'Postmodernity'? • What is a Postmodern Evangelical?
- Theology and (Non)(Post)Foundationalism
- The Bible, Theology and Postmodernism
- Evangelical Faith and (Postmodern) Others
- Postmodern Apologetics • Postmodern Ministry
- Spiritual Formation in a Postmodern Context.
The book is a condensed version of that conversation.

'I know of no better book to introduce readers to this ongoing conversation' – **John R. Franke**, Professor of Theology, Biblical Seminary

Myron Bradley Penner is Professor of Philosophy and Theology, Prairie College, Canada; **Hunter Barnes** is Creative Arts Director for Zarephath Christian Church, in Zarephath, New Jersey.

978-1932805-58-1